D1707629

SINGLE BOOKS IN SERIES

I Found A Baby Bird, What Do I Do?

I Found A Baby Duck, What Do I Do?

I Found A Baby Opossum, What Do I Do?

I Found A Baby Rabbit, What Do I Do?

I Found A Baby Raccoon, What Do I Do?

I Found A Baby Squirrel, What Do I Do?

First Aid For Wildlife, Basic Care For Birds and Mammals

WILDLIFE CARE FOR BIRDS AND MAMMALS

7 VOLUME
BASIC MANUAL
WILDLIFE REHABILITATION SERIES

DALE CARLSON
and
IRENE RUTH

illustrated by
HOPE M. DOUGLAS, M.A.

BICK PUBLISHING HOUSE
MADISON, CT

THIRD EDITION
Edited by Ann Maurer
         Richard A. Alter, D.V.M.

Book Design by Jennifer A. Payne
Cover Design by Pearl & Associates

Library of Congress Catalog Card Number: 96-079851

ISBN: 1-884158-16-1

Printed by McNaughton & Gunn, Inc.

ACKNOWLEDGMENTS

Our gratitude to the network of Connecticut wildlife rehabilitators that includes Connecticut Wildlife Rehabilitation Association, Wind Over Wings members, especially Cathy Zamecnik, founder and director of Little Feet; Dawn and Job Day; Susanne Colten-Carey; Tamara Miglio; Hope M. Douglas, founder and director of Wind Over Wings; Suburban Wildlife volunteers Pam Dickson of We Rescue; Karen; Mary Hollander, founder and director of Pesky Critters; Irene Ruth, founder and director of Suburban Wildlife; Ron Wulff of Wildlife Sanctuary; Laura Simon, president of Connecticut Wildlife Rehabilitation Association.

Our special thanks to Dan Mackey, publisher of Wildlife Rehabilitation Today Magazine, to the International Wildlife Rehabilitation Council, and the National Wildlife Rehabilitation Association for their inspiration and high standards of excellence.

And our thanks to the librarians at ALA and ABA, and to Jan Nathan, executive director of Publishers Marketing Association, who suggested this collected 7-volume book.

CONTENTS

INTRODUCTION

This is not just a book about animals. This is a book about when and how to rescue creatures in distress; basic physical examination for injury; first aid; species and age identification; diets and feeding techniques; basic housing; and general rehabilitation and release techniques. This book will not teach you to be a veterinarian or a wildlife rehabilitator, but it will teach you initially how to help distressed, injured, and orphaned animals, and who to call for professional help.

Rehabilitation is to give back life. Young, orphaned mammals, nursing or newly weaned, have simple yet essential needs for clean, warm environments, specialized formula and diets, and nurturing, surrogate parenting from human caregivers. It is necessary to have a kind heart, but it is equally necessary to know when to leave a mammal nest alone, or a fledgling bird learning to fly, how to rescue properly, examine, feed, house, rehabilitate, and release appropriately.

Rehabilitation is to give back life. The experience of saving life changes people as well as ensures a healthy future for our environment. People ask, why bother to save one small bird or squirrel? A rehabilitator's answer is that we save life because it needs saving, and because it is becoming evident that everything in the universe is connected to everything else, and so everything, no matter how small, matters. A raccoon or opossum has the same life force flowing its small body as we do. When you care for any single creature, you care for all life. Many of the species on our planet are dying out, and if too many of them die, we will die also.

To save a species, you have to save its young. Independent, backyard rehabilitators, many of whom are young people, save wildlife by the thou-

sands and release them back into the wild. Rehabilitators do not take prisoners, but restore and release. They take no pets for their own sakes, but restore and release back to the wild when possible. No matter how attached one gets to orphaned or injured wildlife, to rehabilitate is to raise, nurture, teach, and release. It is also up to us to educate, to teach that whether animals are hurt by nature, deliberate hurting (as if killing for fun were a fully human trait, or it were sporting to kill a defenseless animal), or because we have inadvertently invaded their habitat, it is up to us to help.

Rehabilitators also understand the limits of rehabilitation. Any sick or injured adult, or infant or juvenile, needs to be taken to a veterinarian unless you have the necessary skills.

We can all learn to rehabilitate. Even though helping hurt and distressed animals seems like an easy thing to do, it isn't always as simple as it looks.

Your state, like most states, may require a legal permit to raise and release wildlife, and for most permits, training is required. Call your Department of Environmental Protection (or whatever your state calls its department of conservation) or your Federal Fish and Wildlife Department for advice, for the telephone number of your nearest local rehabilitator, for information on how you can get training and your own permit.

REMEMBER: These skills are for adult use only. Young children should not handle wildlife for their own safety, and the well-being of the animal. It is important for parents, teachers, librarians, and wildlife professionals to teach children how to respect and rehabilitate wildlife. But it is equally important, for the safety, from injury and disease, of both children and wildlife, that only adults handle orphaned and injured animals. Help them to respect and observe what you are doing, but it can be dangerous for children to handle wildlife, and even more dangerous for infant wildlife to be handled by inexperienced hands.

I FOUND A BABY BIRD, WHAT DO I DO?

DALE CARLSON
ILLUSTRATED BY HOPE M. DOUGLAS

CONTENTS

RESCUE

Why Birds Get Hurt

You can come upon hurt and helpless birds in all sorts of places for all sorts of reasons. They can fall or be pushed out of nests in trees. They can get stunned by cars, by flying into big glass windows, or high wires. People shoot and wound them. They get caught in boat propellers, or plastic bags and can connectors. They are killed and sickened by our oil spills, poisoned by our pesticides and toxic wastes. They are hurt not only by our ways of living, but by our domestic pets, cats in particular, and even more by our unwitting invasion into and destruction of their natural habitat.

Sometimes they get hurt by each other or in nature. Orphaned and injured birds are found in towns and in the country, in forests, on beaches, by highways and lakes. But whether it is our fault or nature's fault, people who care save life simply because it needs saving.

Watch, Wait, Warm

These are the key words in rescuing wildlife in distress. The first instinct in people who care is to rush in and save. The trouble with too much haste is that without proper observation and information, you may be kidnapping a bird in no need of rescue.

Watch first for an hour or so unless you see blood or an open wound; or a leg, beak, or wing damaged; or that the bird is cat-caught or uncon-

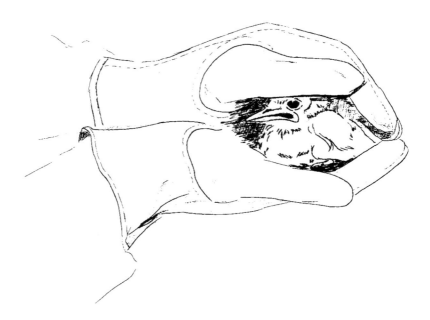

scious. A fledgling or nestling may simply have been coaxed from the nest to teach it to fly. Often the parents have gone for food.

Wait until you are sure the baby is abandoned. Safety for the bird means determining its age, size, and condition. Safety for you means not handling a bird too large for you, or any raptors such as hawks and eagles, by yourself. Call for professional help if you cannot easily hold a distressed bird in your hands. A small bird pecks a little. The claws and beaks of larger birds can be dangerous.

Warm the bird. Make a nest of your hands. Cup the bird to keep it warm, quiet, and in restful darkness. It will be shocked and scared from its fall or accident. Don't be frightened. Now, carry the bird gently in your hands. You will need the help of a licensed rehabilitator to care for the lost baby, even if this is only over the telephone. This is true even more if the bird is hurt.

When your bird is warm, and you find it is unhurt, put it back in its nest if you can. Or make a nest out of a hanging box or planter filled with leaves and hang it near the spot you found the baby. Watch again to see if its mother or father comes back. Most birds have little sense of smell. You can handle baby birds. Parents will not reject them.

It is always a good idea to wear gloves when you pick up birds or any kind of wildlife. Proceed gently but firmly and quietly. Birds stress easily.

If no parent comes after an hour or two, or if the bird is hurt, the situation is now up to you.

DO continue to keep the bird warm.

DO NOT feed it food or water right away.

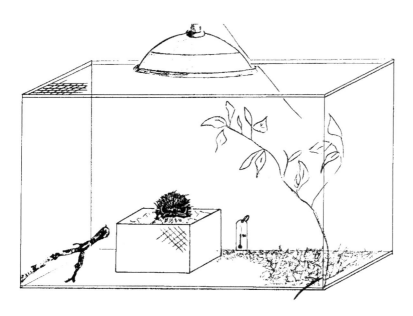

Initial Care

Place the bird in a warm, quiet, semi-dark place. You will need two boxes: a small one for a nest, and a larger one to put the nest inside of.

Make a tiny nest box. A berry box filled with scrunched up toilet paper is perfect. It is important to support a baby bird's body so the bones will grow right.

A cardboard box will do for the larger container. An aquarium tank with wire mesh cover is fine. Line it with paper toweling, an old T-shirt, a piece of sheet. No newspapers for babies, and never colored papers (color is poison).

Put the baby inside the nest and the nest inside the bigger box. Continue to provide warmth with a 60 watt bulb adjusted at 12" to 18" above the nest box. At night, use a 60 watt blue bulb or your bird will be unable to sleep. Do not use Teflon-coated bulbs, as these give off toxic fumes.

Watch now, don't handle. Small birds suffer stress from handling.

First Aid

For first aid techniques, use volume seven of this series. Most immediately, look to see if a wing droops. Look to see if it can't stand on one of its legs. Look to see if there is any bleeding. Watch to see if the bird just lies on its side or breathes through its open bill. You will need help to treat any injury or disease. Call for advice. Call a trained animal rehabilitator if you know one. If not, call your Department of Environmental Protection, or your vet or local police, who will have telephone numbers for a wildlife rehabilitator near you.

REMEMBER:

- DO NOT feed it immediately. Any bird, a baby or adult bird, may eat too much too fast if it's too hungry and go into shock.

- DO NOT OFFER LIQUID. If you offer a drink, even by dropper or in a little shallow bowl, to a baby bird, you risk drowning it by getting fluids into its breathing hole.

- DO GIVE it bits of watermelon, berries, or grape halves to rehydrate, restore body fluids and nourish. Some birds gape naturally. Some beaks you must pry open gently.

Call for help if you cannot easily hold a bird in your hands.

2
IDENTIFICATION AND STAGES OF GROWTH

While your critter is resting and recovering from the shock of its accident or abandonment and rescue, it is a good time for you to identify and learn about what you've got. When you find a baby bird, or one is brought to you, be sure to take notes. Record all pertinent information concerning the bird: where it was found, habitat, tree, or ground; its size and coloration; circumstances such as presence of adult bird screaming or dive-bombing the rescuer. This information will guide you as to species, and especially important, diet. Birds need the correct food, or they will die, even if they eat what you give them and seem full.

Do not overhandle (birds have higher blood pressure than mammals and extreme fright may cause the aorta to rupture and the bird to die). But look carefully. Size, colors, habitat will give you clues as to the species. Check a really good field guide bird book at your public library, if you don't own one. There are many more species of birds than mammals, some 8, 900 in the world, over 800 in North America alone. Birds are designed on the principle of being strong but lightweight. Their skeletal structure consists of hollow bones that provide a strong but light frame. Their limbs are paired: the forelimbs are wings for flying; the hindlimbs adapted for various functions such as perching, wading, grasping, climbing, etc. Their young are divided into four categories:

1. **precocial chicks :** born with eyes open, down-covered, leave nest within one to two days after hatching, either completely

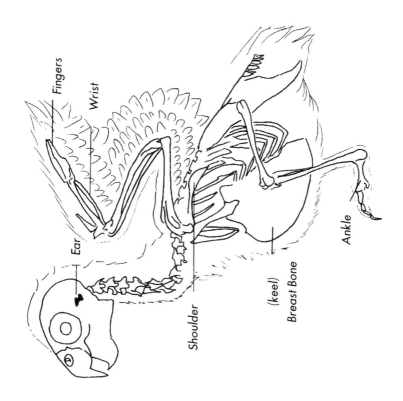

Fingers

Wrist

Ear

Shoulder

(keel)
Breast Bone

Ankle

27

independent or follow parents but find own food like ducks, shorebirds, or are given food (grebes) or shown food (quail)

2. **semi-precocial:** born with eyes open, down-covered, stay in nest, like gulls

3. **semi-altricial :** born with down, but unable to leave nest, some eyes open like herons and hawks, some eyes closed like owls

4. **altricial:** eyes closed, little or no down, unable to leave nest— this includes passerines— songbirds

It is their ability to fly that has given birds a range of habitat greater than mammals. It is their variety that can be confusing. Species, as well as age, is fundamentally important to diet and manner of feeding, and also information as to day or night activity, whether migratory or living in one place year round. These facts are vital to healthy rearing.

Rehabilitators generally divide birds into four groups: songbirds with various diets; shorebirds/waterfowl which eat fish (herons), rodents (loons), cereal grains (swans, ducks, geese); raptors which eat rodents and other small prey; game birds (heavy-bodied, largely terrestrial birds such as grouse, pheasant, quail) which eat grain mixtures. There are also special pellet diets for certain waterfowl, and unmedicated poultry mashes, frozen mice or rats (supplemented), and commercial bird-of-prey diets, though the last are still controversial. Check the appendices of this book for organizations and reading material to find additional information for the diets of shorebirds/waterfowl, raptors, and gamebirds, or call a re-habilitator or the organizations listed.

This book is primarily concerned with caring for small birds. Here is a page of some common songbirds divided into feeding types.

House Sparrow   Hairy Woodpecker

Barn Swallow   Nuthatch

Starling   Morning Dove

1. Aerial-feeding insect-eaters (swallows, swifts)
2. Foliage-feeding insect-eaters (chickadees, wrens, woodpeckers)
3. Ground-feeding insect-eaters (robins, sparrows)
4. Seed-eaters (finches)
5. Omnivores who eat everything (crows, blue jays, starlings, mocking birds)
6. Columbids (rock doves or pigeons and mourning doves)

Along with species, you need to find out your bird's age. Here is a page of birds at different ages and stages of development.

HATCHLING: eyes closed, no feathers: week one

NESTLING: eyes open, hopping, beginning feathers: week 2-3

FLEDGLING: feathered and flying but not self-feeding: 25-28 days

Not only do different kinds of birds eat different food, birds of different ages eat different food. Only the right food at the right time will help birds to thrive.

A NOTE TO BIRD-LOVERS: Do not feed bread to wild birds, songbirds or waterfowl, or shore or game birds. Bread fills them with empty calories and may cause rickets, airplane wing, and other debilitating deformities. A pocketful or bag full of cracked corn is perfect!

And if you're going to fill bird-feeders—do so year round. Don't get wild birds to depend on a food source, build nests for their babies, and suddenly cut them off. And please, bell—preferably house—your cats if you are going to feed birds near your home.

AGES AND STAGES

HATCHLING: eyes closed,
no feathers: week one

NESTLING: eyes open,
hopping, beginning
feathers: week 2-3

FLEDGLING: feathered
and flying but not self
feeding: 25-28 days

3
BASIC DIET

Baby Bird Checklist

1. You have got your bird warm, rested, and calm.

2. You have seen it is not too hurt or stressed.

3. You have given it rehydrating fruit.

4. You have identified your bird and its age in your book.

Feed Your Bird

You have waited for twenty or thirty minutes to allow the bird to rest and recover and warm, and by now it may be looking or sounding or

Where is she?

acting really hungry. It may be gaping (opening its mouth) or peeping (calling) for food.

Emergency Food
You can feed in tiny bits:

1. dry (complete) dog or cat food soaked in a little warm water
2. mushy canned dog or cat food or strained baby beef

Formula for a Baby, Hatchling or Nestling

1/2 cup complete canned dog food or strained baby beef
2 Tablespoons high protein baby cereal
1 hard-boiled egg yolk (3 yolks=1/4 cup) crumbled
moisten with warm water or fruit juice, not milk.

For a 1-4 day old nestling add enough liquid (water or fruit juice) to make a slurry that can be fed with a syringe. For older nestlings add enough liquid to make the mixture the consistency of canned dog food.

Commercial nestling diets are available, including Lafeber's NUTRI-START, Wild Wings PASSERINE DIETS. Use these diets according to instructions.

Adult Bird Diets

Food for your bird as it gets bigger, both fledgling and adult:

    1 part canned dog food, or dog chow soaked in water
    1 part high protein baby cereal with wheat germ
    applesauce
    Make a mush of all these ingredients

Feeding wild birds in captivity is a technique that takes training and skill, as well as a knowledge of species-specific diets. There are manuals listed in the appendices that suggested appropriate diets for all categories of wild birds, but unless you are licensed it is not legal for you to keep the birds. Call for professional help.

How Often To Feed

Baby birds have to eat very often. You will need to feed as often as they need to eat, just the way a mother or father bird does. For baby birds, the general rule is every 20-30 minutes from 7 a.m. to 7 p.m. At 10-14 days old, feed every hour. At 15 days to fledgling, feed every 2 hours.

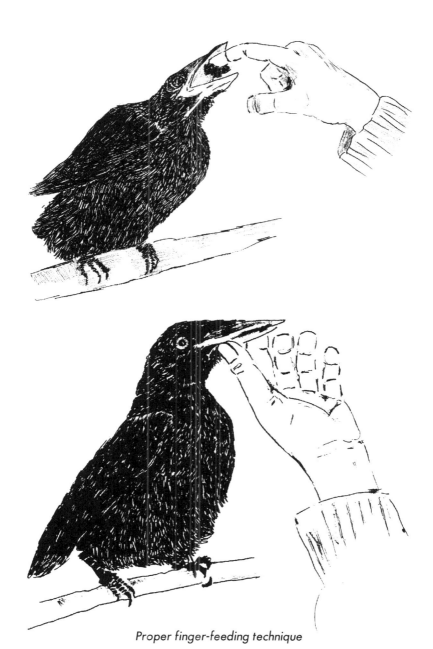

Proper finger-feeding technique

Amounts To Feed

HATCHLING	100% of body weight per day
FLEDGLING	50% of body weight per day
ADULT	feed only morning and evening 25% of body weight per day

When feeding nestlings, avoid over-filling crop so that it is never hard to the touch.

Droppings

Defecation usually follows feeding. Healthy droppings are firm, usually forest green and white for most birds. Songbird droppings are usually brown, but reflect whatever has been eaten, as in berry diets produce purple or red droppings. Our suggested diet will produce brown in variable shades. Bright green or mustard yellow may indicate bacterial infection; diarrhea may be foul-smelling; black droppings or no droppings, digestion problems. Diet and constipation must be corrected immediately, or the bird may die in a short time.

Grit is required for the digestion of many seed and grain-eating birds such as doves, ducks, and geese. Feed grit (necessary for digestion) by sprinkling over food.

Feeding Techniques

For very young birds, use tip of your finger to offer the mush. You can also use a cotton swab without the cotton to push food into the gaping bill, past the glottis, into the throat. Do this very carefully so as not to injure the bird any further. Older birds will eat on their own.

Check Bird Diets

Brukner Nature Center, IWRC, NWRA, and others in the appendix will list diets based on sound nutrition for all species of birds and are periodically updated as needed. Consult your wildlife rehabilitator, and veterinarian, as well, for the special diets of waterfowl and shorebirds and diving birds that include fish; game birds that eat special grain mixtures such as layer pellets or mash, or even better gamebird crumbles; and raptors such as owls, hawks, and eagles who need rodents and other prey food.

There are two main types of small bird diets.

Grain-eaters will eat mixed bird seed.

Insect-eaters will need worms and insect foods. You can buy these dried at most pet stores. Or you can catch them yourself.

Many adult birds thrive on an easy combination of canned dog food, berries, grapes, veggies, sunflower seeds.

Clean the nest and box or cage every day.

Offer fresh food and shallow bowl of water every day. Most song-birds like to bathe every day, in water, sunshine, dust, or a combination of these.

4
HOUSING

First Home

You have already made a small nest from scrunched toilet paper in a berry box or similar container and placed it inside a bigger cardboard box or aquarium or cage. Your baby bird will be fine here as a hatchling, even a nestling.

As your bird grows into a fledgling, juvenile, and adult, in captivity a bird's housing requirements vary according to its size, species, and physical needs. Injured birds in particular need a quiet, private area. Birds recovering from injuries need room to strengthen damaged limbs. Fledglings need sizable flight habitats, plenty of room for preening, bathing, feeding, and flight practice.

Second Home

The International Wildlife Rehabilitation Council (IWRC) and the National Wildlife Rehabilitators Association (NWRA) have both standardized wild animal housing requirements as to species, size, anatomical differences and needs. Just as you would call these organizations for updated diets, you can call them for housing requirements.

To begin with, you will need to build or buy a cage with enough room for hopping. It must have mesh fine enough so your bird cannot fly out or any other animal get in. Fill the hopping cage with things from your bird's original natural environment. Use your field guide and your imagination. Make sure there are perches, branches, and twigs. Put a few dried leaves

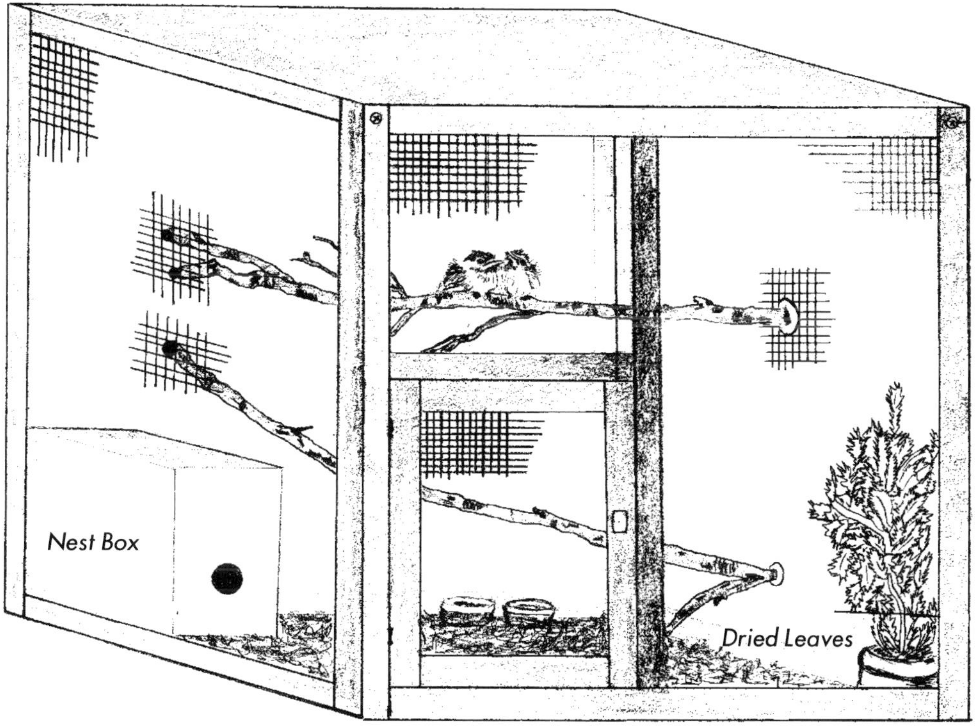

Galvanized or
Brass Screws

Hardware Cloth
Outside

Avian Netting
Inside

Dried Leaves

HOPPING CAGE
(18" x 18" x 18")

Nest Box

39

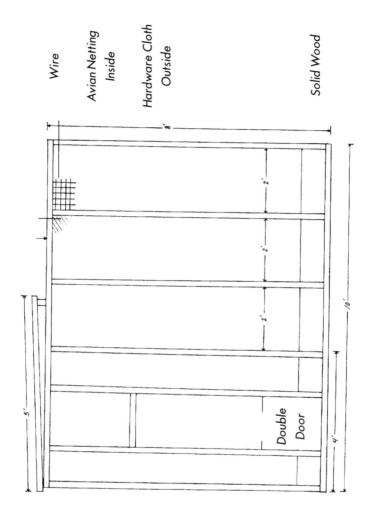

Wire

Avian Netting
Inside

Hardware Cloth
Outside

Solid Wood

Double
Door

8'

2'

2'

2'

10'

5'

4'

FLIGHT CAGE
for small birds view with one door. (see top view)

40

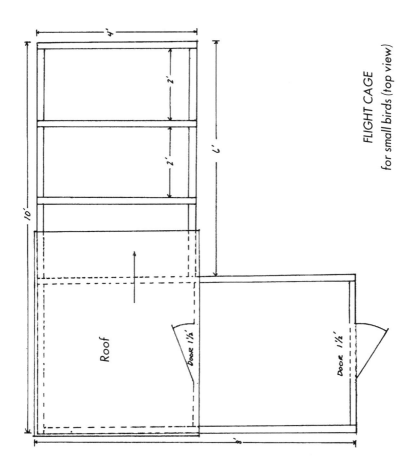

4'

2'

2'

6'

10'

Roof

DOOR 1½'

DOOR 1½'

8'

FLIGHT CAGE
for small birds (top view)

41

in the cage. Your bird will miss the woods or the marsh or the water's edge where it was born.

Please keep your cages clean of old food, feces, too much collected debris. You do not want sickness—or to attract predators by the smell. Most important is that cleanliness keeps diseases and parasites at bay and prevents bacteria and mold. Provide clean water daily for drinking and frequently for bathing so the bird can keep itself and its feathers in good shape.

Third Home

At the juvenile and certainly at the adult stage, a bird's specialized anatomy and needs must be taken into account. By now, you will certainly have contacted a professional or be in training for your own license. Special housing requirements must be understood.

You will need to build a flight cage, or aviary. Have it look like this.

It will have to be tall enough for your bird to fly up in. It will need a flight or nesting shelf for the night with an area of protection from the weather. It will need the right kind of nesting box.

Put in tall, thick, leafy branches to look like a tree, buy potted trees. Put in a food dish. Put in dirt dishes, plants. Put in a water and bath dish. Put thick leaves and pine needles on the floor. Use newspaper underneath for an indoor cage.

Make sure there are plenty of perches at different flight levels.

Do check up on special requirements. For instance: waterfowl need pools for swimming, diving, or wading, and padded floors to protect feet; hawks and owls need padded perches to protect their feet when perching; woodpeckers need vertical logs for climbing and drumming.

There is great pleasure in watching recovering and maturing birds learn to use their wings and develop their skills. Enjoy them. From hatchling to release is only a few weeks.

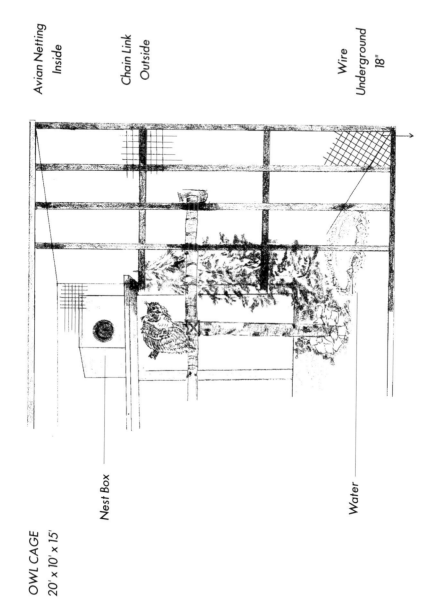

OWL CAGE
20' x 10' x 15'

Avian Netting
Inside

Chain Link
Outside

Wire
Underground
18"

Nest Box

Water

43

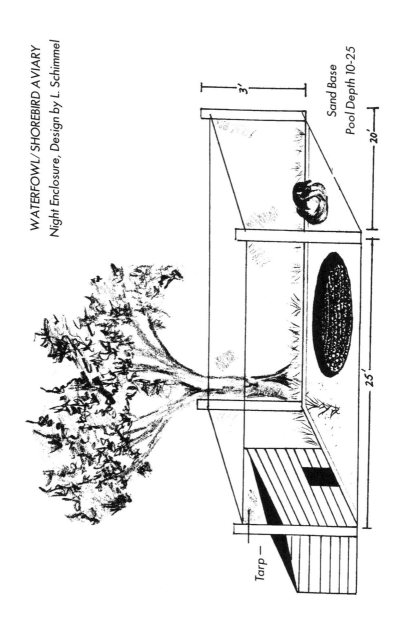

WATERFOWL/SHOREBIRD AVIARY
Night Enclosure, Design by L. Schimmel

Sand Base
Pool Depth 10-25

3'

20'

25'

Tarp —

Companionship

Most birds are lonely by themselves like any other animal. If you can find a bird that is similar, that is the best. If not, certain species such as swans, geese, and other waterfowl can be housed together. So can many types of songbirds. Do watch, however, for personality and gender differences that may provoke attack or prevent proper feeding.

If all you have is the one baby bird, you will have to be its surrogate parent, teach it not only to eat and to fly, but the dangers of household pets and what else to be afraid of, humans in particular. You and your pets may not hurt the bird. Other pets, wild animals, and humans will.

Imprinting, attaching to its own species, is very important. If all your bird sees is you, it will be hard for it to learn to be a bird, to sing the right songs, to learn what to fear, to find food in the wild and mate and nest .

5
RELEASE

Your bird was born free. Rehabilitators do not make prisoners of healthy creatures but release them back into the wild. It is a good idea to check release sites, not only by reading about bird species in their natural habitats, but by talking to local natural resource officials, biologists, other rehabilitators. You will need to find out whether there are similar species in the area (for mating and company and to ensure there is the right kind of food) ; what the area's carrying capacity for the species is (too much competition for mating and feeding); whether there are too many people, roads and therefore cars and cats and dogs, in the area.

Let the bird live in an outdoor flight cage before you release it. Do this for one week before release.

If you live in a city or cannot leave it in an outside aviary, wait a little longer before releasing. After release, leave food out for the bird for a week or two. This will help it not to starve while it learns to find food on its own. After a while, it will no longer return. You will have done a successful release.

Release is the most important part of wildlife rehabilitation once you have saved a life. Wildlife is not ours to possess, only to help in its distress and let go.

It may help to remember the differences between domestic animals who have been bred to live with humans and changed genetically in the process like dogs and cats and cows, and those who have been wrongly imprinted (birds) or tamed or habituated like mammals. Captive animals are originally wild, caught animals whose original nature is unchanged, whose wildness is part of them. We are animals with feelings. So are they. No one wants to live life against its nature.

Sometimes a bird is too injured or too young to survive. Sometimes it cannot or will not thrive in captivity. More than most species, birds mask their pain to deter predators. But a bird may hurt too much and die to release itself. It is not your fault. You did your best. You protected its life and its dying, kept it fed, warmed, and safe from the fear of predators.

You cared.

Growing away is part of rehabilitating.

Grief over release and death is part of rehabilitating. We have discovered the best ways to handle grief is to talk about it with someone appropriate, and then go on to help the next bird.

6
TIPS

Hot Tips for You

1. Don't handle a bird if you don't want to.

2. Call for help and advice.

3. Don't birdnap a baby bird. Watch for parents before rescuing.

4. Your goal in rescuing a bird is its release when possible. No critter wants a life prison sentence unless it's too hurt to survive.

5. Wear heavy gloves for larger birds. They use beaks and claws under stress.

6. Keep any critter away from your face.

7. Wash hands first for bird's sake.

8. Wash hands after handling for your own sake.

Hot Tips for Critters

1. In the case of found babies, watch for parents first: DON'T BIRDNAP while parents are off to find food.

2. Warm bird first in your hands, or against your body.

3. Put in warm, quiet, dark place to recover from shock.

4. It is a good idea to give rehydration fruit before food.

5. Never feed a cold, starving bird before warming and rehydrating.

6. Keep household pets away, however gentle. Birds and other small wildlife need to learn to fear cats and dogs.

7. Call your Department of Environmental Protection or Conservation, or your local wildlife rehabilitator, for advice and help. Your veterinarian or your local police will have telephone numbers.

I FOUND A BABY DUCK, WHAT DO I DO?

DALE CARLSON
ILLUSTRATED BY HOPE M. DOUGLAS

CONTENTS

1. RESCUE

2. IDENTIFICATION AND STAGES OF GROWTH

3. BASIC DIET

4. HOUSING

5. RELEASE

6. TIPS

1

RESCUE

Duck Differences

Ducks are capable of a high degree of independent activity from birth—they are precocial waterfowl like geese and swans—precocious, really. They are born with down (baby feathers); they can see; they can walk; they can feed themselves; and they can swim.

A mother duck lays her eggs in one place, and leads her babies to water. The water may be anywhere from a few yards to a mile away. This means baby ducks can keep up, on land and in water, from birth. In a newly hatched duck, the egg tooth that helps it to break out of its shell is noticeable, both vision and hearing are well developed at hatching, its legs are fully functioning.

This is not to say you just stick a baby duck in the water and let go.

Baby ducks are amazing. But they are still baby ducks. The wings are still small and undeveloped; they are unable to fly at hatching. Despite their downy covering, precocial chicks do not have full temperature control until they are 4 weeks old and will become chilled if they are away from the nest too long.

They need care.

Watch, Wait, Warm

It is always important to understand the nature and habits of creatures in the wild to determine a true orphan and to help it properly.

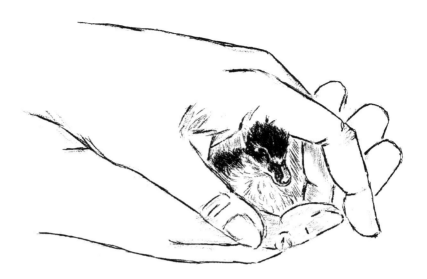

Ducklings are seldom abandoned unless the mother is killed. Unlike some other species, the mother does not wander away from her young to feed. However, a duckling may wander away from the family.

Wait to see if it peeps and the mother comes back to find it. A duckling may also get lost and frightened and separated from the group in crossing a road.

Watch for some time to determine whether the family reunites.

If a pet or your child brings you a baby, try to find the mother and the sibling ducklings. You will know your area, and the waters where you have spotted similar species. Put the duckling back with the others. If you spot more than one group, keep trying to place the duckling near them in turn. Some mothers will reject a strange baby, other mothers will take on an extra baby with no problem.

Once you are sure your baby's family cannot be found, or you know the mother is dead, CARE BEGINS.

Warm the baby duck. Make a nest of your hands. Be careful the duckling does not jump out of your hands.

Don't be frightened. A baby duck doesn't bite.

If you find baby ducklings, and there is no mother, scoop up the babies who will run in all directions. Scoop them into your shirt as if you were collecting berries. As soon as possible, put them into a box or carton— make air holes— and keep the lid on tight. Remember, ducklings are precocious!

You will need the help of a licensed rehabilitator to care for the baby duck or ducklings. This is true even if you are a practiced rehabilitator of other species but without experience with ducks. This is true even more if the duck is injured or has symptoms of severe dehydration or disease.

DO keep it warm.

DO NOT feed it food or water right away.

Duck under teddy and light in simple brooder.

Initial Care

Place your baby duck or ducklings in a warm container in a quiet area.

At first, a cardboard box with a tightly taped lid and airholes will do. If you have a piece of wire mesh for the top of your box, this is good. Even better, a simple brooder can be made using a 10-gallon aquarium with a wire mesh cover. Either place this on a heating pad under 1/2 the aquarium or place it under a 60 watt bulb 12" to 18" above. Do not use Teflon-coated, so-called shatterproof bulbs as these give off toxic fumes. Line your brooder with diapers or soft cloth, paper toweling or sand, but not newspaper. Newspaper pulls the oil, the duckling's waterproofing, from the feathers.

It is particularly important to keep your dog and cat away from the baby duck. They should not become used to pets. It is equally important to make certain the baby duck can't jump out of whatever housing it is in.

Put a stuffed animal or feather duster in with the ducklings to simulate a mother duck and to give them something to hide under or behind. If you have a single baby, put in a clock with loud ticks to simulate the mother's heartbeat. Sand is necessary for both digestion and to give a natural feeling to your habitat. Grass and leaves, chemically untreated, of course, provide both natural environment and, later on, food.

Light

For ducks, light is crucial for warmth. Clamp your 60-watt-bulb in a metal shade to the side or simply rest it on the wire mesh cover of the box or aquarium. This is better for ducks than the heating pads often used underneath for baby mammals because the temperature is more evenly distributed over and around them, not just underneath them.

NOTE: At night, use a blue bulb. This will keep the baby duck warm and also allow sleep.

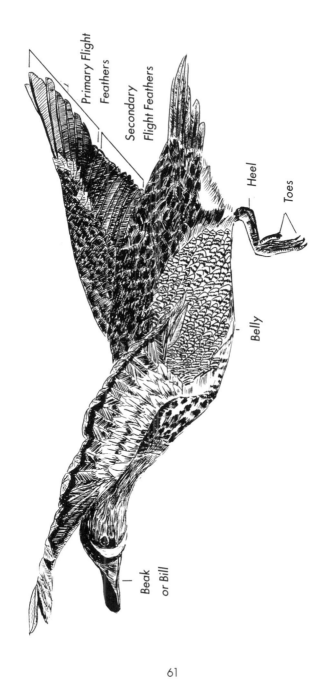

Primary Flight
Feathers

Secondary
Flight Feathers

Heel

Toes

Belly

Beak
or Bill

61

Clean box or aquarium twice each day.

Watch now. Except to check for dehydration, let the baby rest. To check for dehydration, examine legs for wrinkling and sunken eyes.

Single ducks attach themselves to human beings very quickly. This is called imprinting. So that this does not occur, give your single duckling as much privacy and handle as little as possible. Clearly, it is better to raise ducklings with each other for company, not you.

First Aid

For first aid techniques, use volume seven of this series. First, look at your duck to see if it seems hurt. Look to see if the legs are working properly and turned in the right direction. Look to see if it can't stand properly or one of its legs seems paralyzed. Look to see if there is any bleeding from an external wound. Look to see if blood flows from nose holes or bill to indicate internal bleeding. See if your duckling seems weak. Watch for discharge from eyes.

Call for advice. Call a trained rehabilitator if you know one. If not, call your Department of Environmental Protection, or your vet or local police, who will have telephone numbers for a wildlife rehabilitator near you.

REMEMBER:
DO NOT feed your duck immediately, not until it is warmed and a bit rested from the shock of rescue.

If it is weak, give rehydration fluid orally. Severe dehydration requires a vet's subcutaneous injection. When your baby duck is warm, use a small plastic dropper, syringe with or without the nipple, to give the following special drink called a rehydrating solution. (Never do this with a cold animal.)

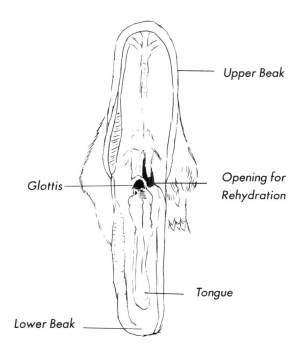

Upper Beak

Glottis

Opening for Rehydration

Tongue

Lower Beak

Carefully, squeeze three drops of rehydrating solution into a duckling's throat beyond breathing hole at base of tongue. **See Illustration**. This is done every fifteen minutes for the first two hours. If it is responding nicely to this, do it every forty-five minutes.

Go slowly. Don't miss and go into the lungs. This causes aspiration, or inhalation pneumonia.

1 teaspoon salt		1/3 teaspoon salt
3 Tablespoons sugar	or	1 Tablespoon sugar
1 quart warm water		1 cup warm water

The above is a homemade solution. Commercially available electrolyte solutions such as Pedialyte or Lactated Ringer's solution can also be given.

Let your duckling rest quietly under its lamp in between rehydration feedings.

2

IDENTIFICATION AND STAGES OF GROWTH

Look at your duck again carefully. Then look at a really good field guide wild bird book. You will find a good book at your public library if you don't own one. Do not forget to take notes. Record the circumstances of the rescue, as place, habitat, conditions will be important to care and release later on. This information will also guide you as to type of duck and its proper diet. **Waterfowl—ducks, geese, swans—need the proper diet to thrive and avoid debilitating deformities.** They spend all their lives on or near water. They nest, breed, feed on or near wet areas. Nesting usually takes place from April to July, with clutches of 5-16 eggs. The female builds the nest and lines it with vegetation and with down from her breast. Incubation is 27-34 days, depending on the species. Within 12 to 25 hours, the young are led to water. They fly at 50-70 days old. Unlike fish-eating shore birds like gulls, or marsh birds like herons, waterfowl eat vegetation and cereal grains. Most waterfowl migrate south for the winter. Rehabilitators and the organizations listed in the back of this book will give you additional information about ways to identify your type of duck, its diet, habitat, and needs, as well as other birds in all four groups: songbirds; game birds; raptors; other waterfowl/ shorebirds.

Here is a page of some common ducks.

1.   Lakes and ponds: mallard, wood duck, merganser
2.   Sea: scoter, eider
3.   Marsh: muscovy

Mallard

Northern
Shoveler

Common
Goldeneye

Redhead

White-Winged
Scoter

Hooded
Merganser

66

Ages and Stages

You need to find out your duckling's age to feed it the proper diet and house it in the proper way.

Here is a page of ducks at different ages and stages of development.

- **Infant:** down-covered, eyes open, tiny wings

- **Juvenile:** 3 weeks to one month, down and feathers, longer bill, webbed feet bigger

- **Adult:** at 50 to 70 days, ducks can fly, adult feathers and coloration, fully developed wings

Ducks from different habitats eat differently. The wrong food fed wrongly will not help your duck to thrive properly.

A NOTE TO BIRD-LOVERS: do not feed bread to wild birds, songbirds or game birds, shorebirds or waterfowl. Bread fills them with empty calories and may cause rickets, airplane wing, and other debilitating deformities. A pocketful of cracked corn is perfect. In really cold winter weather, a whole bag of cracked corn is even better!

Infant less than one week old

Mallard Juvenile

Adult Mallard Female

3
BASIC DIET

Baby Duck Checklist

1. You have got your duckling warm, rested, and in its proper housing.

2. You have seen it is not too hurt or stressed.

3. You have given it rehydration fluid.

4. You have identified your baby duck and its age in your book. You have identified its habitat in order to feed it correctly., You understand its natural environment, natural habits. All of this will help you care for it better.

Feed Your Duck

You have waited for twenty minutes to allow the duck to rest and recover and warm, and by now it may be looking or sounding or acting hungry. You begin by mixing its food, just as you would for any baby animal. Food for the baby duck (also baby geese and swans) is a mixture of the following:

1 cup UNMEDICATED poultry mash or commercial waterfowl ration pellet diet like Manna Pro (buy at feed store)

1/2 cup water

2 drops vitamins

1 Brewer's yeast tablet

1 hard-boiled egg yolk crumbled, shredded spinach, cooked, mashed carrots for first three weeks

Also feed a variety of other chopped greens besides spinach , such as kale, clover, watercress, or even cooked spinach fettucini (if you're up to it!) Also give, in small bowl, 1/2 cup of high-protein, growth, canned dog food Also offer berries, watermelon, and if you wish, scoop up some pond greens for your duck

Make certain your duckling has a container of water in its habitat. In the beginning, for the first two weeks, this water is only for drinking and may be offered in a shallow dish no more than one inch in depth so your duckling does not drown. An excellent way to offer water is in a large mason jar inverted over a special feeder lid (available at pet and farm stores), making sure the lid is small enough so the baby duck cannot get into the water. But be sure it is never empty. Your duckling needs water to drink.

Food dishes should be non-tippable, so that when ducks walk through them, they will not spill. Amount of food should be limited to what is consumed in four hours, as ducks will defecate, get water in food. Change food at least twice a day. Offer natural foods from the wild.

Amount to feed: 50% of body weight as chicks, daily.

Juvenile and Adult Duck Diets

Feed 10% of body weight daily to adult ducks. (Feed geese and swans 5%.) Decrease water in feed mixture gradually over a two week period until ration is dry. By week 4, begin switching over gradually to adult diet; by week 6, dabbling duck chicks should be on adult diet of commercial waterfowl ration pellets supplemented with 25% cracked corn and mixed grains (wheat soybeans, wild rice, poultry pellets, waterfowl pellets, oat groats). Or the following mixture:

40% cracked corn

20% trout pellets or fish food

40% mixed grains

Add a handful of coarse grit (pet or grain store) sprinkled over the feed several times a week for adults, as well as chopped greens, grated raw carrots. You can offer mealworms several times a week.

(For diving ducks, give 50% raw fish, 50% trout pellets supplemented with thiamin and Vitamin E; for wood ducks 10% corn, 25% trout pellets or fish food, 55% grain mixture.)

REMEMBER your duck is self-feeding. Limit dog food to half a cup a day for each duckling, but replenish everything else.

Mallards and wood ducks are the most common in rehabilitation. A single wood duck may not eat well alone. You can try putting a wood duck in with a mallard if you happen to have one of each of approximately the same size. Obviously be sure that they get along and won't injure each other.

The chick diet does not vary for the approximately fifty to seventy days you will have them in captivity before they can fly and it is time to release. For an injured juvenile or adult, the above diets are sufficient.

Check Bird Diets and Feeding Techniques

Brukner Nature Center, IWRC, NWRA, and others all listed in the back will list diets based on sound nutrition for all species of birds and are updated as needed. Consult your wildlife rehabilitator, and veterinarian, as well, for any further specialized needs of waterfowl and shorebirds and diving birds.

Clean

Clean the brooder every day.

Make sure the food is fresh.

Make sure the water is fresh, to assist birds to maintain their waterproofing. If water is contaminated by food or feces, birds can become wet and cold in water. Also remember to gauge the depth properly: a baby cannot get out of even three inches of water when it is very small.

First Home

You have already made a small home in a cardboard container with a wire mesh lid or an aquarium with a wire mesh cover. You have a lamp with a 60 watt bulb clamped 12" to 16" above it for warmth. This is excellent for the first three weeks. Do clean twice a day, as unsanitary conditions can quickly cause serious, often fatal, diseases.

Second Home

At three weeks, as the ducklings grow, their down changes into feathers, and their wing and feet size increases. Remove the warming lights and give your duck or ducklings a larger home to allow for exercise, preening, bathing, and all other activities.

Now a four by six foot outside habitat is required.

Predator-proof wire cages should be made of 1/2" hardware cloth with avian netting on inside to protect feathers. Avian netting over the hardware-cloth bottom permits feces and soiled food to drop through and is forgiving to the ducklings' feet. A wooden floor is harder to clean. Do not have wire mesh flooring under a duck's feet.

Water is now important to your duckling. While still in the aquarium, at two weeks old, take your duckling for a bath in your sink in water only deep enough for your duckling to stand in. **Ducklings should not be left unattended in the water at this stage.**

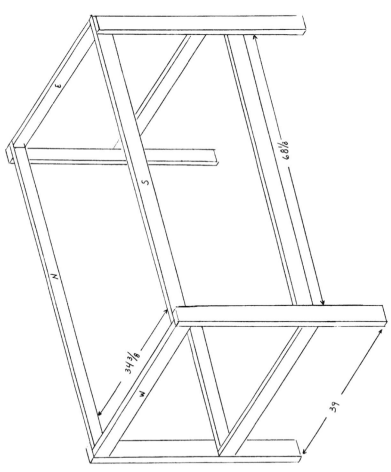

Frame for Cotton Net Cage - 2 doors on south side, one door on west side. Wire mesh 3' x 30' around outside and underneath. Frame avian netting as floor.

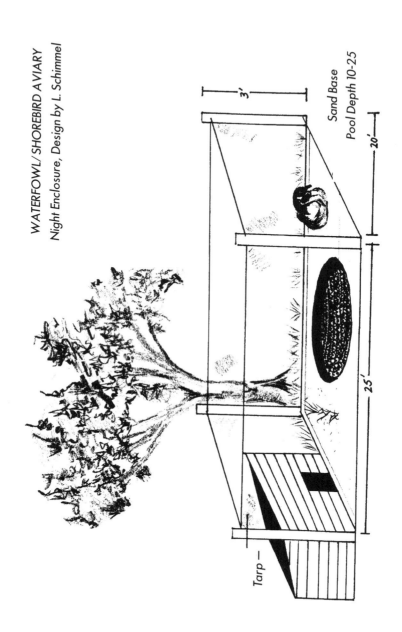

WATERFOWL/SHOREBIRD AVIARY
Night Enclosure, Design by L. Schimmel

Sand Base
Pool Depth 10-25

3'

20'

25'

Tarp —

In the outdoor cage, a tub, a flat pan, like a kitty litter pan, should be filled with clean water daily. Be sure your duck can get in and out of the pan at will. A stepping rock may help.

Put in branches, a cup of gravel for digestion, a pet carrier for protection from weather and for privacy in one corner of the habitat. Add a separate container of water for drinking to the various food dishes.

Predators

A note about predators other than raccoons or members of the weasel family. Rats can chew their way into most habitats. They are attracted to the water and feed of wildlife. In disproportionate numbers, they became a danger. While it is true rehabilitators save life, they must sometimes make the difficult decision to balance populations of rats and save infants from rat attack by calling an experienced exterminator to remove safely or at least contain a too-fast growing rat population. Disease and attack are threats to other animals, and even to the rehabilitator, the rehabilitator's home, and family. A difficult choice, but it is sometimes a necessary one.

5
RELEASE

At fifty to seventy days, your ducklings are ready for release. Their wings have developed. They're getting off the ground a bit. Their feathers are waterproofed because the ducks are preening naturally now. You can tell the feathers are waterproof. When water gets on their feathers now, it beads. Your ducks are getting adult colors—check your field guide book—and they have grown into their beaks.

They appear restless in captivity.

You have not imprinted them on any household pets or yourself.

They have been conditioned to outside temperatures.

It is time for letting go.

Your ducks were born to swim free.

You have taught them all they need to live free, about what to eat and who to fear.

Make sure the weather forecast is good for at least three days.

Release in the morning.

Make certain that there are other similar ducks at the release site so that you know there is proper food for your ducks to eat.

Release, if possible, away from people and motorboats.

It is up to you to decide on the best environment for them, but your decision will be based on conversations with local wildlife rehabilitators and conservationists about the safety and carrying capacity for ducks.

If you have raised your ducks to the point of release, you have done a successful rehabilitation. But remember the when and where of the release is the most important , after the saving of life to begin with.

Wildlife needs to be safely returned to the wild.

Your ducks may grow strong and when released swim out of your life into their own. But if they do not thrive and grow strong, if they are too injured and die, it is not your fault. You did your best to protect them in life and death, kept them fed, warmed, and safe from predators.

As a rehabilitator, you need to share your grief over missing them when released or of having them die despite your tender care. And you will learn over and over again to help your own grief by helping the next creature in distress.

6
TIPS

Hot Tips for You

1. Don't handle a duck if you don't want to.

2. Call for help and advice.

3. Don't ducknap a baby duck. Watch for mother before rescuing.

4. Your goal in rescuing a duck is its release when possible. No critter wants a life prison sentence unless it is too hurt to survive.

5. If you find an injured adult duck, wear gloves.

6. Keep any critter away from your face.

7. Wash hands first for duck's sake.

8. Wash hands after handling for your own sake.

Hot Tips for Ducks

1. In the case of found babies, watch for mother first: DON'T DUCKNAP while mother is looking for a peeping baby duck.

2. Warm duckling first in your hands, or against your body.

3. Put in warm, quiet place under the light of a 60-watt-bulb.

4. Generally, it's a good idea to give rehydration solution before food.

5. NEVER FEED a cold, starving duck or any other critter before warming and rehydrating.

6. Keep household pets away, however gentle. Ducks and other small wildlife need to learn to fear cats and dogs.

7. Call Department of Environmental Protection, or your local wildlife rehabilitator, for advice and help. Your vet or local police will have telephone numbers.

I FOUND A BABY OPOSSUM, WHAT DO I DO?

DALE CARLSON

ILLUSTRATED BY HOPE M. DOUGLAS

CONTENTS

1. RESCUE

2. IDENTIFICATION AND STAGES OF GROWTH

3. BASIC DIET

4. HOUSING

5. RELEASE

6. TIPS

1
RESCUE

Why Opossums Get Hurt

Most of the young opossums rehabilitators receive come to us because the mother has been killed on the road. Opossums get roadkilled because they freeze in terror—lie down to seem dead when threatened—and because their eyes don't focus quickly and headlights paralyze them. When the mother is hit, the young stay with her instead of scampering. The only home the infants know is in her pouch. When they are older, they cling to her back. Either way, they will rarely leave her body. These young opossums will either be roadkilled with her, be alive in her pouch, or thrown. If their mouths are still sealed (there is only a small opening that attaches to the mother's nipple), they have only the smallest chance of survival even in the hands of a rehabilitator.

Opossums travel alone night after night in search of food. They eat everything: frogs, worms, corn, grass, birds, crayfish.

Because humans have invaded their habitat, they enter backyards to share our garbage or leftover dog food. The wooded areas and quiet streams they once claimed have turned into our crowded suburbs. We are now the most dangerous enemy the ancient opossum has ever had. When it isn't our cars, it's our territoriality that kills, our guns, traps, and poisons that maim and kill them. Opossums are clean, nonaggressive, nondestructive. They are immune to many diseases, not likely to carry rabies. They are quiet, reclusive animals beneficial to the environment because

The opossum has been around for 60 million years, since the days of the dinosaurs. It is North America's only marsupial, like Australia's kangaroo and koala.

they eat insect pests. The opossum has been around for 60 million years, since the days of the dinosaurs. It is North America's only marsupial, like Australia's kangaroo and koala. Help this creature survive.

Watch, Wait, Warm

Any young opossum you find, new born or infant up to 75 days, you will probably find near a roadkilled mother. Unlike other mammals, opossums do not leave their young to forage, but carry them inside the pouch or on their backs. There is no need to wait and watch. Warm your baby opossum in your hands (wear gloves), until you can place it on a towel-wrapped hot water bottle in a pet carrier, or in a cardboard box lined with soft cloth or nonstringy toweling placed 1/3 of the way over a heating pad turned low.

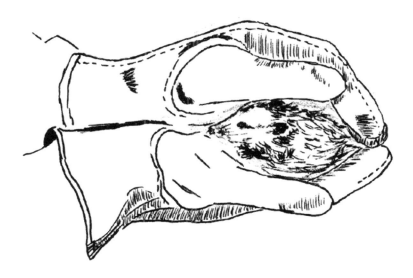

Initial Care

It is important, in the case of opossums, that you place a moistened sponge or wash cloth inside the container. Moisture is absolutely necessary to maintain humidity for opossums to prevent the animal's tail from drying and sloughing off. The mother's pouch normally provides moisture. Baby oil on the tail also helps.

It is also important to prepare an artificial pouch from soft cloth with one end sewn shut, 12"L x 16"W. Use flannel or something like a sweat pants leg or sleeve. Anything rougher may rip the baby's toenails.

You will soon need to construct double-decker housing for baby opossums, but the box will do for the moment until you get advice and help.

The whole arrangement should be placed in a quiet area, away from bright lights, household pets, and noise. The baby needs to recover from the shock of its removal from its mother, a new environment, and being taken care of by a strange species—you.

Call your Department of Environmental Protection, your vet, your local police station, to find the name and number of a wildlife rehabilitator in your area. This is particularly important in the case of opossums, because they are much more difficult to feed and care for than other mammal babies.

If there is only one baby, place a ticking clock in the box to simulate the mother's heart.

Don't be frightened. Even experienced rehabilitators are cautioned to wear gloves when picking up young opossums because of the startle effect of their vocal sounds: opossums hiss, click, growl, and screech when threatened, even before they bare their teeth or assume the position of death. (The death position, by the way, is an instinctive physiological reaction to fear. It is not a game.)

While you let your baby or babies rest, look up opossums in a good animal field guide. To rehabilitate well, it is important to understand wildlife in the wild. The adult opossum is about the size of a cat, with a coat

Opossums have opposable thumbs.

consisting of long, white hairs covered by black-tipped fur. Adult opossums have long noses, large naked black ears with pink tips. The tail is prehensile, but with apologies to B. Potter, opossums hang by their feet. The tail is used for balance, to carry nesting material. Out of 20 or so in the litter, only 13 will survive because the opossum has exactly 13 nipples. The young stay in the mother's pouch for 10 weeks, then sleep together in the nest or ride on the mother's back when she forages, attached to her tail by theirs. The babies are weaned and independent at about 10 weeks in the wild. Adults are 12-20 inches long. They possess 50 teeth, more than mammals. They have opposable thumbs. Their lifespan is 2-7 years.

Remember to call: you will need the help of a licensed rehabilitator to care for the babies. This is true even if you are a practiced rehabilitator of other species but without experience with opossums, especially if an opossum is injured or has symptoms of dehydration or illness.

First Aid

You will need to do a basic physical examination to see if your opossum is hurt (see volume seven of this series). Look to see if the limbs are placed properly in relationship to be the body, not bent or twisted or

93

hanging limply. Look to see if a limb drags or is crooked. Look to see if it can't stand properly or one of its legs or both seem paralyzed. Look to see if there is any bleeding from an external wound, if blood flows from nose or mouth to indicate internal bleeding. Watch to see if your opossum just lies there or its breathing is rough. Watch for runny bowel movements. (Healthy baby feces on a milk-based diet are soft, but formed, and yellowish in color; weaned, the stool is formed, solid, brown.) Watch for discharge from nose or eyes.

Check for and remove with fingers any external parasites, like fleas, mites, or ticks.

You will need veterinary care to treat any injury or disease. Opossums, while immune to many diseases, may have flatworms, roundworms, tapeworms, and other endoparasites. Metabolic bone disease can result from improper diet.

IMPORTANT NOTE ABOUT FEEDING OPOSSUMS: Not only is the moisturized, double-decker housing different for an opossum than other animal babies, the process of feeding is different as well. Opossum babies do not have a sucking reflex like most mammals. There are two methods of feeding. If you are experienced or under the supervision of an experienced rehabilitator, you can tube-feed with a French size 3 1/2 feeding tube and urethral catheter using a 1cc syringe for infants up to 75 days. If you are not experienced, *on no account tube feed.* You will use an eye dropper or syringe, and leave the stomach tubing out. Be careful, whatever feeding tools you use, not to aspirate (get formula into the lungs) as this causes a pneumonia condition.

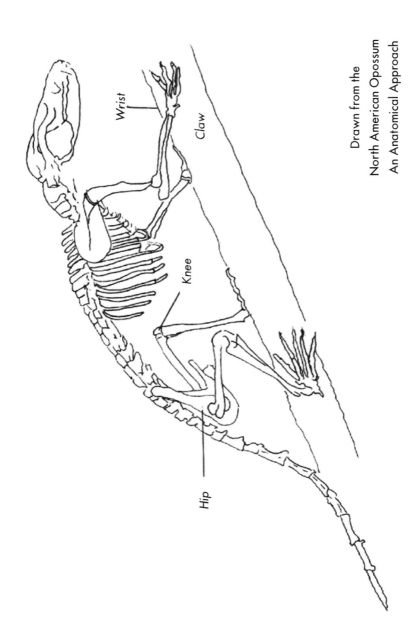

Wrist

Claw

Knee

Hip

Drawn from the
North American Opossum
An Anatomical Approach

REMEMBER:

DO NOT feed your baby yet. Baby opossums will react to a change from mother's milk to your formula. Also, they are usually dehydrated. Pinch to tent the skin. If skin is slow to return to normal position (greater than 1-2 seconds), your babies need rehydration. (Severe dehydration needs a veterinarian's subcutaneous injection of Lactated Ringers solution.)

DO give even healthy babies a special drink first called a rehydrating solution. Generally, a rehabilitator will be confronted with six or eight opossum babies. To tell which ones have been fed, we use two pouches, depositing the newly fed babies into the second pouch (ski caps work).

MIX:

1 teaspoon salt		1/3 teaspoon salt
3 Tablespoons sugar	or	1 Tablespoon sugar
1 quart warm water		1 cup warm water

The above is a homemade solution. Commercially available electrolyte solutions such as Pedialyte can also be given.

Give this orally the first three feedings at least, offering 1/4-1/2cc every fifteen minutes over the first hour. If dehydration is present, you may want to continue feeding the rehydration solution for the first 24-36 hours every two hours after the initial rehydration. Remember, in the case of very immature opossum babies, their chances of survival are slim. If they are mostly furred and their mouths are open (this happens at 2 months), they stand a better chance.

Make certain your babies are kept warm and make certain you moisten the cage sponge each feeding time. Some opossums sleep much of the time, see that your babies rest quietly and in a semi-dark place in between feedings to reduce stress.

QUIET is the watchword for babies.

2
IDENTIFICATION AND STAGES OF GROWTH

You need to find out your opossums' age to feed it the proper diet and house it in the proper way. Check your wildlife animal field guide for information on the growth stages of opossums.

Here is a page of opossums at different stages of development.

Infant: Embryonic young are the size of a kidney bean or a bee, weigh 2 grams, and make their way up the abdomen to the pouch and attach to 13 nipples. Eyes and ears closed; they are furless. At 2 months, mouth and eyes open, they are covered in fur, they are 2 inches long (excluding tails). They let go of the nipples, leave the pouch for brief periods, return to the pouch to feed. Generally, they ride on their mother's back, but may be left in the den occasionally.

Juvenile: At 70-75 days, teeth erupt. Weaning is at 10 weeks. At 3-3 1/2 months, they are independent.

Adult: Female opossums are sexually mature by 6 to 7 months, males are mature by 8-9 months. In captivity, opossums can live up to 7 years. In the wild, they live 1 1/2 to two years. Their home range shifts. They hear and smell acutely. They eat anything, plant or animal. Nocturnal, they are solitary except during mating.

Your opossum babies need different foods at different stages to help them grow properly.

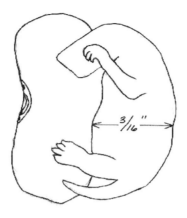

Newborn opossum and kidney bean.

Juvenile opossum.

Adult opossum

3
BASIC DIET

Baby Opossum Checklist

1. You have got your opossums warm, rested, calm.

2. You have seen they are not too hurt or stressed.

3. You have given them rehydration fluid.

4. You have identified your opossum's age in your book and read as well about its natural habitat, natural foods, natural habits. All of this will help you care for your baby or babies better. Most important is to check diets and feeding techniques with professionals.

Feed Your Opossum

You begin by mixing formula, just as you would for any baby animal. The baby opossum's formula is closest to a puppy's. We use Esbilac. Before the eyes are open, leave out the cereal and applesauce.

This is the formula we are using currently. Mix:

2 parts water

1 part Esbilac (or use other puppy replacement formula powder and mix according to manufacturer's directions)

1 part baby rice or oatmeal or high-protein cereal

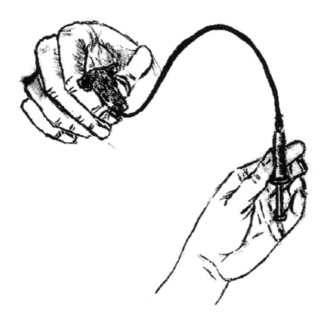

1 part applesauce (pure, no preservatives)

Theralin (vitamin and mineral supplement) (amount according to package directions, powder or liquid)

Be careful of aspiration. If necessary, even before the eyes open, thicken formula with more cereal. Be careful of bacteria. Wash syringes and other feeding tools thoroughly between feedings. Make enough formula only for a twenty-four hour period. Hold baby upright or on its stomach to feed: never on its back.

You can ask your veterinarian for Nutri-Cal, a high caloric, dietary supplement for any babies who do not seem to thrive or have much appetite. It comes in a tube, tastes good, stimulates appetite.

Chilling can occur rapidly with baby opossums, so wrap them or feed quickly and return them to the warmth of the pouch. Older opossums will click, looking for food, and drool.

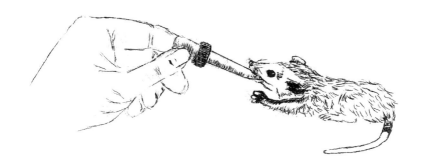

Feeding Chart

Joeys under a month are nearly impossible to keep alive. Formula at this stage needs to be given a drop at a time. You will need a gram scale to weigh your baby.

OPOSSUM WEIGHT

10 grams	.52 cc's every 4 hours
25 grams	1.03 cc's every 4 hours
50 grams	1.74-2.35 cc's every 4 hours
	(2 months and still smaller than your little finger)
100 grams	5 cc's every 4 hours

Gradually increase the amount as the infant's appetite increases.

Adolescent: at 70-75 days, begin the weaning process by placing a small, shallow lid of Esbilac in the cage and dip animal's nose into formula. It should begin lapping at the food. You can feed a whole litter at the same time. Keep refilling the lid until they've all stopped eating. Make certain each opossum is full. You might also feed in a separate area as opossums are messy eaters and will walk through food. Clean them with warm water after eating, but make certain no one gets chilled.

IMPORTANT: Until eyes open, you must stimulate elimination and urination as opossum mothers do. Gently rub the genital region with moistened cotton ball or tissue. Keep the water warm by remoistening. Or use a dry cotton ball but rub very lightly. Discontinue stimulation after two minutes whether elimination has occurred or not. You must do this until it becomes obvious babies are eliminating and urinating on their own. For bloat, submerge the lower body in warm water, and massage it for about five minutes, making sure afterwards to dry baby off. Dilute or alternate formula with rehydration solution. If bloat continues, see volume seven of this series. Never overfeed: tummy should be round and firm as a marshmallow, not tight.

Weaning: At 10 weeks or so, when you begin to offer the lid of formula, also begin adding natural foods—diced apples, insects, eggs, fruit. Also offer canned dogfood with high protein cereal, or dog kibble with formula poured on to moisten it. Offer a bowl of water at all times.

REMEMBER: by 12 to 16 weeks, your opossums should be ready for release. For the days before release, feed at dusk. Your opossums are nocturnal and need to be reminded to feed at night.

4

HOUSING

First Home

A lidded, Rubbermaid plastic box makes an excellent incubator for opossum babies. Drill holes in the top. Place a thick towel on bottom, cover with flannel cloth for babies to crawl under. The thermometer should read 95 degrees F. Place a moistened sponge (remoisten each feeding) inside box. Place heating pad underneath 1/2 of box, set on low. The pouch you have made may also be used inside the box.

Second Home

When the eyes are open (60 days) and the babies are more active, make the following cage. Use 2 cardboard boxes, so that both light and dark areas for burrowing are provided. Place a towel in the bottom of the lower box. The lower box has a lid. Cut a hole in the lid and in the bottom of the upper box so babies can climb from one box to the other. Drape a towel under the lid of bottom box for climbing up to holes. In bottom of upper box, use kitty litter, paper, leaves so they defecate and urinate there, as they do not like to soil their sleeping place.

Place a screen or 1" hardware cloth bent securely on top of the top box. Clean the top box often and place the food up there as opossums are messy eaters.

Adolescents (75 to hundred days) are eating on their own and are completely furred. A 3' x 3' x 3' cage is recommended with wire size 1".

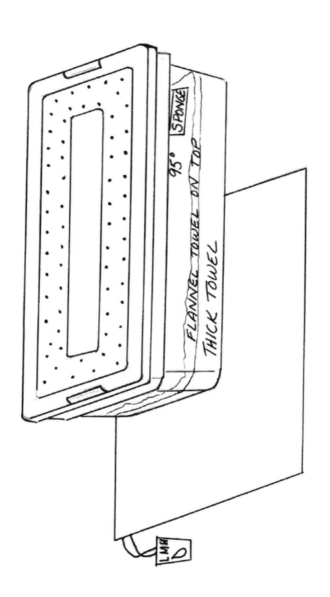

SPONGE

95°

FLANNEL TOWEL ON TOP

THICK TOWEL

L MH

106

SECOND HOME

Two Cardboard Boxes

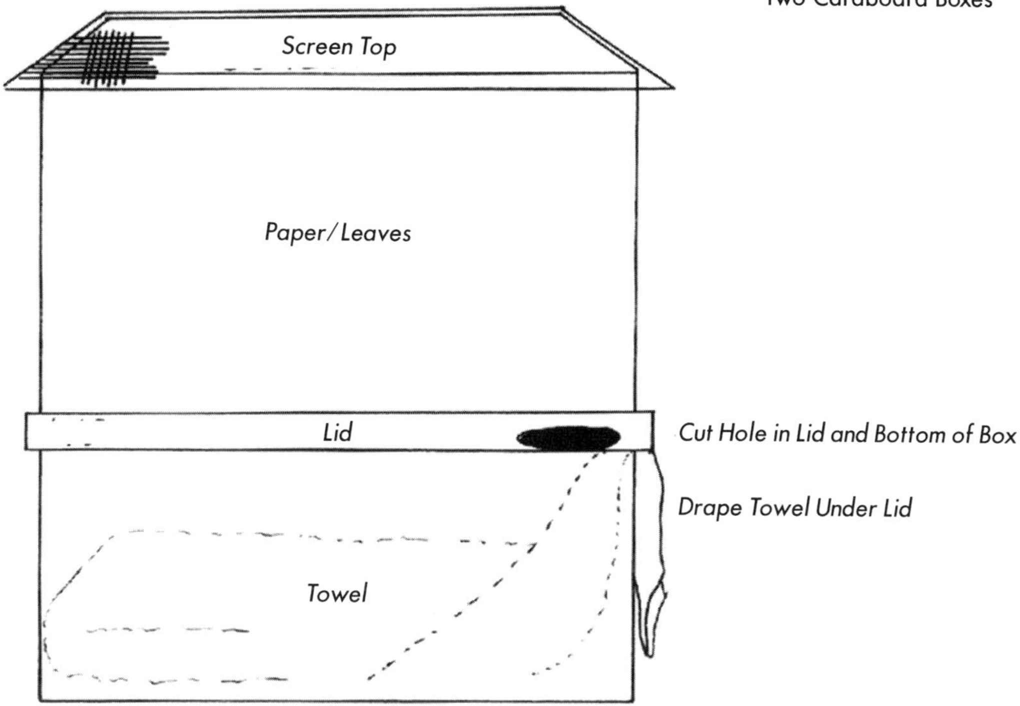

Screen Top

Paper/Leaves

Cut Hole in Lid and Bottom of Box

Lid

Drape Towel Under Lid

Towel

The tray below the cage should have newspaper and litter. You can tie a hammock into the corner of the cage or use a nest box inside cage for privacy. If necessary, a heating pad can be draped over cage for warmth.

Third Home

At 3 months, opossums cannot be overcrowded, as they may quarrel and injure, even kill and eat each other. At this stage or even a little earlier, opossums should be acclimated to outside temperatures before they are released. An outside habitat 4' x 6' x 8' of 2' x 3's and 1" hardware cloth is recommended. Plants, branches, hollow logs, grasses will represent a natural environment. Make sure there is a nesting box, and hammocks.

Again, remember about your domestic animals: Keep them away from your opossums, not for their own sake, but for the sake of your wild creatures. You are not only nurturer, but teacher. You don't want your opossums approaching other people's pets after release and getting hurt or shot. Also, because there is something about opossums that tames easily, do not handle after weaning. Let them learn to avoid you and all humans, just as they learn to avoid pets.

5
RELEASE

Before release at 3 1/2 months, the opossums should have been out-doors and eating totally on their own for at least two weeks. By now, you will be feeding them at dusk. They should be 7" to 10" long, exclusive of tail. Make certain they are no longer friendly, and hissing, teeth-baring behavior is present when you approach too closely.

Check the weather forecast to make certain you have good weather for at least three days.

Release sites should be as far away as possible from humans, and their cars and roads. There should be running water or lakes or marsh rivers. There should be woods for cover and nesting sites, trees to climb to escape predators. The site should be far away from hunting sites. Do check with local biologists and rehabilitators about safety and carrying capacity and conspecifics (others in the same species).

Place temporary food supply, an open 25-pound bag of dry cat or dog food, in a sheltered place near release site. Opossums are nocturnal. Release at dusk.

Grief

One or more of the opossums may not thrive, may be too immature or sick or injured, and die. Grief over the deaths of such little, vulnerable creatures is natural. Even grief over just letting them go, and worry over what can happen to them out there is natural. All you can do is feel it, and move on to help other creatures in distress.

6
TIPS

Hot Tips for You

1.   Don't handle opossums if you don't want to.

2.   Call for help and advice.

3.   Don't opossumnap a baby opossum. Watch for mother before rescuing.

4.   Your goal in rescuing an opossum is its release when possible. No critter wants a life prison sentence unless it is too hurt to survive.

5.   If you find an injured adult opossum, wear gloves when handling.

6.   Keep any critter away from your face.

7.   Wash hands first for opossum's sake.

8.   Wash hands after handling for your own sake.

Hot Tips for Opossums

1. In the case of found babies, although normally mother opossum doesn't leave them, it can happen that she is off a little way looking for food. Watch for her before taking babies.

2. Warm orphaned opossum in your hands, or against your body.

3. Put in warm, quiet place.

4. Generally, it's a good idea to give rehydration solution before food.

5. NEVER FEED a cold, starving opossum or any other critter before warming and rehydrating.

6. Keep household pets away, however gentle. Opossums and other small wildlife need to learn to fear cats and dogs.

7. Call your Department of Environmental Protection, or your local wildlife rehabilitator, for advice and help. Your veterinarian or local police will have telephone numbers.

I FOUND A BABY RABBIT, WHAT DO I DO?

DALE CARLSON
ILLUSTRATED BY HOPE M. DOUGLAS

CONTENTS

1

RESCUE

Why Rabbits Get Hurt

Most rabbits nest on the ground. They get hurt from: people trampling over their nests; attacks by cats and dogs; people driving lawnmowers into their homes. They are hunted by people with guns, and killed with people's pesticides. They are too quick, mostly, for roadkill by cars.

Nature helps. Raccoons prey on rabbits. So do hawks, owls, ferrets, and a variety of larger predators. Storms wreck their nests. Too much rain drowns. Too little parches.

But whether it is we or nature who hurts them, they need our help.

Watch, Wait, Warm

If you find a nest of babies, watch it first.

To rehabilitate well, it is important to understand wildlife in the wild. Rabbits are wilder than most other critters, and must be understood in the wild to be helped properly.

Before the birth of a litter, the mother prepares a nest in the earth, usually lining it with grass and fur plucked from her own abdomen. The doe often stays away from her babies in the nest, so as not to draw the attention of predators. She watches them from some distance. AN ABSENT MOTHER IS NORMAL — DO NOT BUNNYNAP UNTIL YOU ARE SURE THE BABIES ARE ORPHANED. Remember, too, that rabbits are nocturnal and feed from dusk to dawn, so the mother will often be away even at night.

But she will return on and off all night. At dusk, take two sticks and cross them in an X over the nest. If they are disturbed in the morning, the mother has returned, if undisturbed, the babies are orphans. The mother has been killed.

If a pet brings you a single baby—baby rabbits do not often wander from the nest on their own—first try to find the nest.

IMPORTANT NOTE: Young rabbits who are able to be on their own are small. Do not try to capture any rabbit the size of your fist or larger. Any attempt to round one up will likely give it a heart attack from shock and it will die. If you have to chase it, it probably doesn't need to be rescued!

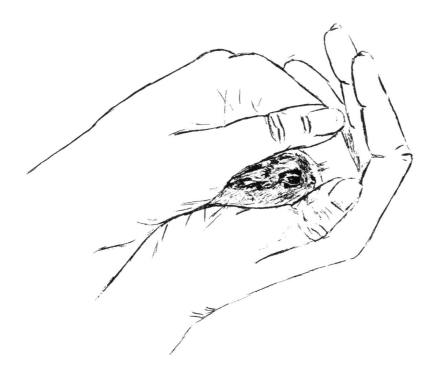

Once you are sure your small rabbit is motherless and too little to be on its own, CARE BEGINS.

Warm the baby. Make a nest of your hands. Be very careful to keep the baby covered as baby rabbits are like coiled springs and will squirt out of your hands if they are startled. Unlike other mammals, baby rabbits should *not* be cuddled because they go into shock so easily. Handle them as little as possible.

A sad warning: orphaned and injured rabbits are difficult to raise and release and their death rate in captivity is high.

Don't be frightened. A baby rabbit doesn't bite.

Initial Care

If you find a nest of babies, scoop up some of the bedding of grass and fur and carry it with the babies in your hands. Or go and bring a small box with a cover. Line the box with paper toweling or a soft, unstringy cloth and some of the original bedding material for familiarity. For the sake of cleanliness, you will discard this after twenty-four hours. Be sure the box has breathing holes. Be sure to cover the box and tape it securely. Even young baby rabbits jump!

You will need the help of a licensed rehabilitator to care for the baby. This is true even if you are a practiced rehabilitator of other species but without experience with rabbits. This is true even more if the rabbit is injured or has symptoms of severe dehydration or disease.

DO keep it warm.

DO NOT feed it food or water right away.

STIMULATE as soon as you can: rub cotton ball or tissue gently over genital area so that eyes-closed babies urinate. This prevents not only discomfort but toxicity.

Place your rabbit, or rabbits, in a warm, quiet, semi-dark place. You will need two boxes: a small box for a nest, and a large one to put the nest inside of.

Make the nest box out of a small wooden or cardboard box, with the opening at one side. Line this with a soft cloth. Or you can simulate the original nest by using two washcloths: one folded up with a depression in it and the other laid over the top. It is important for the rabbit baby to have a dark, private place to be in.

At first, a cardboard box will do for the larger container. An aquarium with a wire mesh cover is fine. Line it with paper toweling, or an old T-shirt or clean flannel cloth or piece of sheet. Never colored newspaper (poison), and no shredding towels (to catch nails or choke in). It is important besides to use white material so you can see when the babies begin to urinate on their own.

It is particularly important to keep your dog and cat away from the baby rabbit. It is equally important to make certain the rabbit can't jump out of whatever housing it is in.

Put the baby inside the nest, and the nest inside the large container. Later, when the eyes are open, you can add leaves and clover and grass for your rabbit to use as nesting material, as well as small leafy limbs for cover, bark, twigs, whatever its original natural environment suggests.

As the rabbits become larger, the size and depth of the box must be adjusted. Rabbits can jump unbelievably high at an early age, and because they hate captivity, will jump at the sides of whatever box or cage or aquarium you keep them in. Hang cloth—cut up bedding pads are excellent—on the inside walls of the housing for padded protection.

Now, continue to keep your baby warm. KEEP IT WARM BUT NEVER HOT! A heating pad turned low under 1/3 to 1/2 the nest and up the side of the outer box will be fine. Keep all heating appliances outside the outer box. Inside, it should feel warm to the touch, cozy, not hot.

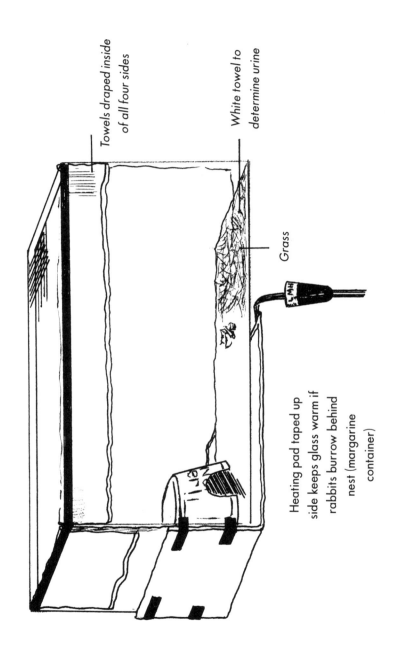

Towels draped inside
of all four sides

White towel to
determine urine

Grass

Heating pad taped up
side keeps glass warm if
rabbits burrow behind
nest (margarine
container)

Clean the habitat once a day.

Watch now. Except for tenting the skin to check for dehydration, let the baby rest. To tent, pinch skin at base of neck. If it takes more than 2 seconds to return in place, your baby is dehydrated.

Hard as it is, stay away from baby bunnies altogether except to clean and feed. This is partly not to stress them. This is also not to habituate, get them used to, human noises, or they will lose their main defense as adults: running at noise.

Two reminders about cottontails: they are prone to stress and fractures; and it is normal for them to eat their own nighttime feces during the weaning stage which contain vitamins and minerals necessary to the health of the rabbit.

Rabbits do not adjust well to captivity and scream, grunt, or growl when threatened.

First Aid

Look at your rabbit to see if it seems hurt (see volume seven of this series). See if the limbs are placed properly in relationship to the body, not bent or twisted or hanging limply. Look to see if a limb drags or is crooked. See if it can't stand properly or one or more of its legs seem paralyzed. Look to see if there is any bleeding from an external wound, if blood flows from nose or mouth to indicate internal bleeding. Watch to see if the rabbit just lies there or its breathing is rough. Watch for runny bowel movements. (Healthy rabbit droppings are hard, the darker the better. Pale green stools means trouble.) Watch for discharge from nose or eyes.

Check for and remove with fingers any external parasites.

You will need help to treat any injury or disease. Call for advice. Call a trained animal rehabilitator if you know one. If not, call your Department of Environmental Protection, or your vet or local police, who will have telephone numbers for a wildlife rehabilitator near you.

A proper holding technique

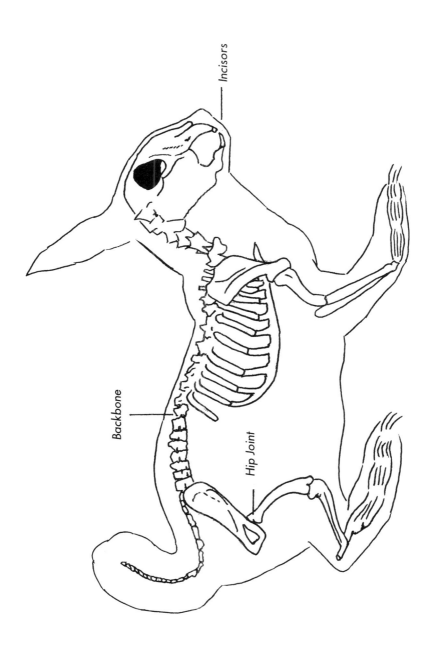

Incisors

Backbone

Hip Joint

REMEMBER:

DO NOT feed your bunny yet. If there is dehydration, give rehydration fluid orally. Severe rehydration requires a vet's subcutaneous injection. Even if the baby rabbit does not seem dehydrated, give rehydration fluid as a good transition from mother's milk to your replacement formula for the first few feedings.

When your bunny is warm, use a small plastic dropper, syringe with or without the nipple, or a pet nurser, to give the following special drink called a rehydrating solution. (Never do this with a cold animal.)

Squeeze a drop or two at time into the bunny's mouth. Wait until it is swallowed. Go slowly and gently to prevent aspiration, or inhalation pneumonia. This can happen when the baby sucks the fluid in up its nose.

1 teaspoon salt		1/3 teaspoon salt
3 Tablespoons sugar	or	1 Tablespoon sugar
1 quart warm water		1 cup warm water

The above is a homemade solution. Commercially available electrolyte solutions such as Pedialyte (baby formula section of the supermarket) or Lactated Ringer's solution (prescribed by a veterinarian) can also be given.

Offer 1cc or 2 cc's every two hours.

Remember: always stimulate genital area so eyes-closed babies can urinate.

Let your rabbit rest quietly in between rehydration feedings.

QUIET is the most important word for rabbits. They have been known to bruise their eyes, hurt their backs, hit their heads and break their necks on the top of their housing in a panic stampede.

2
IDENTIFICATION AND STAGES OF GROWTH

Look at your rabbit again carefully to find out what kind of rabbit you have. Then look at a really good wildlife mammal field guide. You will find a good book at your public library if you don't own one.

Here is a page of some common rabbits

1. Cottontails: Eastern, Mountain, Desert, New England
2. Brush rabbit, Pygmy rabbit, Swamp rabbit, Marsh rabbit
3. Blacktail jackrabbit, European hare

Identifying animals is important to housing and feeding and releasing them properly. You also need to find out your rabbit's age to feed it the proper diet and house it in the correct way.

Here is a page of rabbits at different ages and stages of development.

Infant: naked, eyes closed, ears flat, 3-4 inches long

Juvenile: a week to ten days, fully furred, eyes open; 2 to 3 weeks investigating greens, soft solids, sometimes lapping formula

Adult: 3 to 4 weeks, weaned from bottle, eating greens and solids, ready for release even if the white spot has not disappeared, 4-5 inches long, very afraid of humans

Different aged bunnies eat differently. The wrong food fed wrongly will not help your bunny to grow properly.

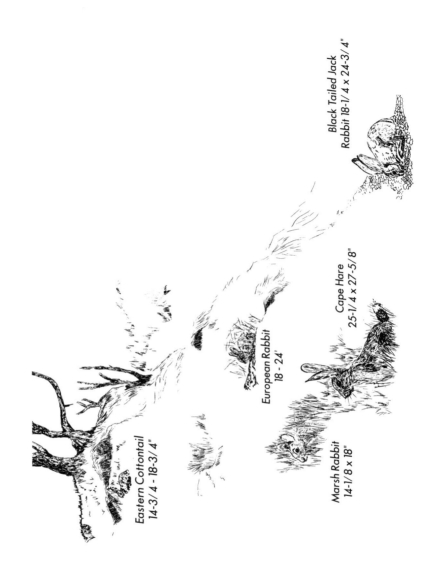

Black Tailed Jack
Rabbit 18-1/4 x 24-3/4"

Cape Hare
25-1/4 x 27-5/8"

European Rabbit
18 - 24'

Marsh Rabbit
14-1/8 x 18"

Eastern Cottontail
14-3/4 - 18-3/4"

Infant: naked, eyes closed, ears flat, 3-4 inches long

*Juvenile: a week to ten days, fully furred, eyes open; 2 to 3 weeks
investigating greens, soft solids, sometimes lapping formula*

Adult: 3 to 4 weeks, weaned from bottle, eating greens and solids, ready for release even if the white spot has not disappeared, 4-5 inches long, very afraid of humans

3
BASIC DIET

Baby Rabbit Check List

1. You have got your bunny warm, rested, and calm.

2. You have seen it is not too hurt or stressed.

3. You have given it rehydration fluid.

4. You have identified your baby rabbit and its age in your book and probably read as well about its natural habitat, natural foods, natural habits. All of this will help you care for it better. You have numbers to call for advice about correct diet and feeding techniques.

Feed Your Baby Rabbit

You begin by mixing formula, just as you would for any baby mammal. The baby rabbit's formula is a little different from that used for infant squirrels, raccoons, woodchucks, because its intestinal environment is different. There are disagreements about formula components and how often to feed baby rabbits. This is what we are doing currently. Mix:

3 parts boiled water

1 part Esbilac powder

2 parts heavy, whipping cream

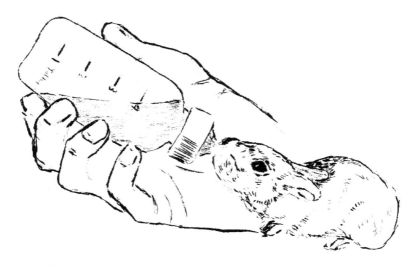

3 drops liquid vitamins per cup formula (Theralin)

Bactrim .02 ml 2x per day for first week to reduce bacteria, to prevent diarrhea, is given <u>before</u> feeding.

When starting formula, do it gradually.

3/4 parts rehydration solution, 1/4 part formula
1/2 part rehydration solution, 1/2 part formula
1/4 part rehydration solution, 3/4 part formula

If your bunnies are not thriving on this, you may substitute one cup of cow's milk, 4 tablespoons of cream, two tablespoons of rice cereal, and a half-teaspoon of maple syrup, but you must use the vitamins and the Bactrim for supplement and to sterilize the gut. Some rehabilitators prefer to use a pinch of lactobacillus acidophilus powder (1/4 of a capsule) rather than Bactrim. Some rehabilitators use Multimilk (Pet-Ag), Unimilk (Manna Pro), or LAMA Lamb Milk Replacer with lactobacillus culture. Mix formula according to label instructions.

For infant bunnies whose eyes are still closed, a plastic dropper or syringe with nipple may work better than a pet nurser. You can control the flow better—never more in the mouth than is being swallowed to prevent aspiration.

Amount to Feed and How Often

Weigh your rabbit and calculate 25% of the rabbit's weight. This is the amount to feed per day. Feed in a sitting position to prevent formula from being aspirated into lungs.

You will hear controversy among rehabilitators about how often to feed. We feed every six hours three times per day from 7 a.m. to 11 p.m. when the bunnies' eyes are closed. Pink hairless bunnies eat 1/2 cc of warm formula every three hours, 6 times per day. Bunnies with closed eyes and flat ears will eat about 2cc per feeding. Increase amounts as the bunny grows from 2 cc's to 5 cc's per feeding. Start to wean from the bottle at three weeks, by eliminating one feeding at a time, the middle one first. They should be weaned by the time they are three to four weeks old.

IMPORTANT. For the first week, stimulate your bunny's genital area after feeding so it can urinate. Unless stimulated, a bunny may die. Stimulate by rubbing area gently with a damp tissue or cotton ball or Q-tip. They may leave their pepper-like droppings on their own, but wait until you see signs of urination on their cage flooring before stopping the stimulation.

To avoid stress during this procedure, stimulate only for a minute and stop, whether they urinate or not.

IMPORTANT. Never overfeed. A bunny's tummy should be full and round—not tight. Like a marshmallow.

Introduce solid foods when the eyes are open. Offer rolled oats, commercial rabbit pellets, fresh greens like clover, dandelion greens, wild carrot greens, alfalfa hay, twigs and bark to chew, fruit tree leaves and blossoms— they love wisteria leaves and blossoms— leafy lettuce, apple bits, sunflower seeds, corn, carrots. Rabbits need balanced diets that include grain, fruit, balanced rabbit feed.

Add a small jar cap of water to the cage during and after weaning. Provide fresh water daily. If they do not seem to drink, sprinkle the veggies and fruits with water. A pan of dirt for dust baths has been suggested in some manuals. And keep leafy branches and grasses about to provide cover for your rabbits as they will frighten more and more easily.

Remember: at 3-5 weeks, your rabbit should be off formula, onto solids, and ready for release. RABBITS HATE CAPTIVITY.

For an injured adult, the food assortment is the same as for a weanling: 80% rabbit pellets and 20% varied mix of rabbit browse food. Rabbits will consume the soft fecal pellets produced at night. This is a good way to obtain nutrients that are only released after the food is digested. Adult rabbits consume about 5% of their body weight per day. Give half the daily ration in the morning, half in the afternoon, although pellets may be provided for nibbling round the clock. Provide salt spools in the habitat, and remember fresh water daily..

4
HOUSING

First Home

You have already made a small nest burrow, a box with tissues, or small, clean cloth inside it, and placed it inside a larger container, aquarium with wire-mesh cover, hardware-clothed dog crate, or a wire carrying cage under 1/3 of which you have placed a heating pad set on low. This is excellent for the first two weeks. Do replace the tissues with clean ones whenever dirty, as unsanitary conditions can quickly cause serious, often fatal, diseases. The heating can be removed when the bunnies are furred and eating on their own.

Second Home

As the rabbits grow and open their eyes at about two weeks of age, caging must be enlarged, to give more room for movement and more space for food, and to help alleviate stress. Two eyes-open bunnies may be caged in an 18" pet carrying cage; three or four (litter is 4-5) in a 2'x 3' and 18" high cage. Always be careful to keep covers on cages as well as when handling, as rabbits startle easily and can hurt themselves jumping suddenly from cage or rehabilitator's hands.

Wire cages could be made of dog crates covered with 1/2" hardware cloth. Cage bottoms must be flush to prevent leg injuries, or put newspaper (no color) on floor grid. And, as previously mentioned, hang soft, padded cloth to inside walls and top to prevent banging injury when bunnies leap from sudden fright. Cover bottom of cages with non-shredding or paper toweling or sheeting over newspaper. Remember, provide lots of hiding places and cover. Leafy branches are good. Or piles of grass.

Try not to mix bunny groups. Fighting may occur. It is always better to bring up baby rabbits with one or more of their own kind. However, if you do mix two or three from different groups, watch them carefully for the first twenty-four hours.

Wire
Mesh

PRE-RELEASE HOME
wire crate covered with hardware cloth

139

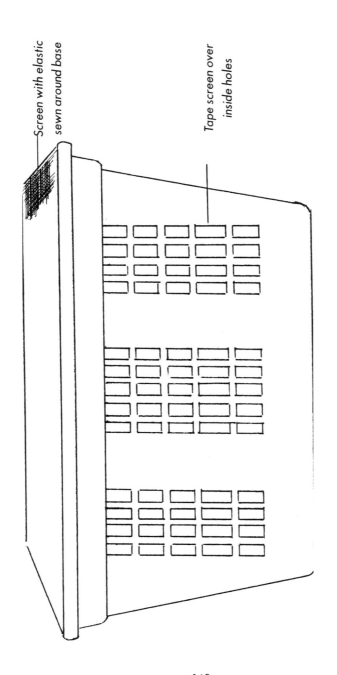

Screen with elastic sewn around base

Tape screen over inside holes

LAUNDRY BASKET HOME
nest box inside, branches, greens

5
RELEASE

DO NOT keep healthy rabbits after five weeks.

At five weeks old or so, your rabbits are ready for release. They are not full-grown, but they are able to care for themselves and do not do well in captivity now. You are no longer handling them. For one thing, they squirt from your hands. For another handling scares them, sometimes literally, to death.

They are self-feeding.

You have not habituated (gotten them used to) any household pets or yourself.

You have conditioned them to outside temperatures by leaving their cage outside during the day for three days.

They are going crazy in their cage, anyway.

It is time for letting go.

You have taught them all they need to live free, about food and enemies—just about everything, in the case of bunnies.

Make sure the weather forecast is good for at least three days.

Release in the early evening or early morning.

Leave rabbit pellets at release site, although rabbits probably will not come back as squirrels and raccoons do.

Release in a location where there are plenty of grazing areas plus wooded areas for shelter. Log piles, thorny thickets, shrubby areas are good sites. Release away from humans, dogs, and cats, roads, gardens. Close their cage after the release if it is nearby, so they cannot get back in and possibly be trapped by predators.

It is up to you to decide on the best environment for them, after you have checked with various other rehabilitators and local specialists in conservation and biology to make certain of the carrying capacity for the area, development plans, and natural predators.

But if baby rabbits are alive and healthy, and you release them into a safe environment, you have done a successful rehabilitation.

Your rabbit may grow strong and when released hop away into a life of its own. But rabbits, almost more than any other creature, hate captivity, and may not thrive. You may lose many of them in your efforts to keep any of them alive. Just know that you did your best, that you cared, that you fed them, kept them warm and safe from predators. Just as your joy is natural in release, your grief over the loss of small lives is natural. It is part of rehabilitation, and as always, its main cure is to help the next small life you can.

6
TIPS

Hot Tips for You

1. Don't handle a rabbit if you don't want to.

2. Call for help and advice.

3. Don't critternap a baby rabbit. Watch for mother before rescuing. Never rescue a rabbit the size of your fist or larger, unless it is injured. You can shock it into a heart attack.

4. Your goal in rescuing a rabbit is its release when possible. No critter wants a life prison sentence unless it's too hurt to survive. Rabbits can get suicidal, especially in captivity.

5. If you find an injured adult rabbit, wear gloves.

6. Keep any critter away from your face.

7. Wash hands first for rabbit's sake.

8. Wash hands after handling for your own sake.

9. Remember, as soon as possible, to stimulate the genital area of an eyes-closed baby rabbit for urination by rubbing area gently with cotton ball or tissue.

Hot Tips for Rabbits

1. In the case of found babies, watch for mother first: DON'T CRITTERNAP while mother is watching from a distance or off finding food.

2. Warm rabbit first in your hands, or against your body.

3. Put in warm, quiet, dark place to recover from shock. In rabbit's case, handle always as little as possible.

4. Generally, it's a good idea to give rehydration solution before food.

5. NEVER FEED a cold, starving critter before warming and rehydrating.

6. Keep household pets away, however gentle. Rabbits and other small wildlife need to learn to fear cats and dogs.

7. Call Department of Environmental Protection, or your local wildlife rehabilitator, for advice and help. Your vet or local police will have telephone numbers.

I FOUND A BABY RACCOON, WHAT DO I DO?

DALE CARLSON
ILLUSTRATED BY HOPE M. DOUGLAS

CONTENTS

1
RESCUE

Why Raccoons Get Hurt

Raccoons get hurt from our attitudes about raccoons. Because we perceive them as a nuisance, we kill them. When they come in out of the cold to nest in our chimneys or garages, we trap, shoot, or poison them. When we suspect, even without cause, that they carry disease, we fear and persecute them out of ignorance and without information.

Raccoons are intelligent, friendly, and curious. They are willing to share. They fight only to defend their nests and their young.

At times, raccoons are killed by predators or disease. Nature kills enough creatures.

Learn to cap chimneys. Learn to deal effectively and intelligently with whatever problems wildlife may present. Learn to live with our wildlife and share the land with them. It can be done.

Watch, Wait, Warm

If you come upon baby raccoons on the side of the road, in a hollow log, under a porch, or anywhere else without their mother, watch before you touch them.

To rehabilitate well, it is important to understand wildlife in the wild. In the case of raccoons, the mother may be nearby, or away feeding herself. Contrary to what people think, although raccoons are nocturnal,

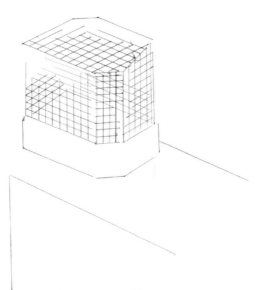

Learn to cap chimneys.

raccoon mothers are often out during daylight hours looking for food. Daylight sightings of raccoons are normal. This is not a sign of anything wrong.

Raccoon babies often wake and leave the nest in daylight to search for their mother if she is gone too long. If you find babies by the road, put on heavy gloves, scruff them (pick them up as you would a kitten by the skin on the top of the neck), and move them back away from the traffic.

Wait and watch. If no mother returns, collect the baby or babies—using heavy gloves, or if you do not wish to touch them, a small shovel—into a covered box.

Call your Department of Environmental Protection for the telephone number of a wildlife rehabilitator in your area.

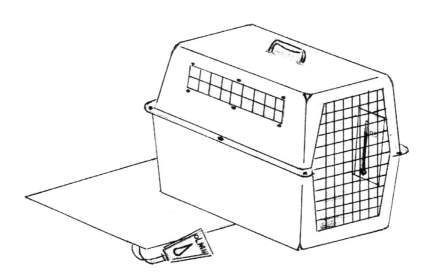

Initial Care

In the meantime, warm your babies. You can keep them in the cardboard box. You can transfer them into a pet carrier, or stainless steel caging unit like a dog cage. Place a heating pad set on low beneath one third of the box. Line the container with paper toweling, but never colored newspaper (poison), and never cloth that shreds (to catch nails or choke in). Put a nonravelling towel, T-shirt, flannel cloth, or ski hat inside carrier to make the nest cozier for your frightened raccoon orphans to crawl into or under.

Later, at four to eight weeks, you will need a larger space, a cage unit 3'W x 3'L x 3'H for three or four kits in which is placed a smaller nest box of wood or cardboard for them to hide and feel secure. And raccoons love to play and climb. Hammocks, ramps, leaves, small branches create fun and a natural environment. (Remember: because of roundworm, do not use cage, nestboxes, toys, or anything else you have used in the care of raccoons for the care of any other creatures.) If there is only one baby, place a ticking clock inside a piece of cloth to simulate the mother's heart.

Don't be frightened. Baby raccoons won't bite you.

DO keep your baby raccoons warm.

DO NOT feed them food or water right away.

Place your box of baby raccoons in a warm, dark, quiet place. Don't handle for a while. Let them rest. It is particularly important to keep the family dog away from the baby raccoons. For proper release, dogs must remain natural enemies.

Call: you will need the help of a licensed rehabilitator to care for the babies. This is true even if you are a practiced rehabilitator of other species but without experience with raccoons. This is true even more if a raccoon is injured or has symptoms of dehydration or illness.

Companionship

In the case of a single baby, try to locate a companion. Unlike rabbit and squirrel mothers, raccoon mothers will often spend a year or more with their babies nurturing and teaching them. Raccoons are affectionate and sociable animals, and they need one another for company, to learn from, and for nurture, both in rehabilitation and afterwards in the nocturnal hours of their release. A companion will also lessen the temptation of the rehabilitator to become attached to the baby raccoon. It is better to encourage these intelligent, sociable, and affectionate animals to become attached to and to depend on each other.

First Aid

Look at your raccoon to see if it seems hurt. Check volume seven of this series. Look to see if the limbs are placed properly in relationship to the body, not bent or twisted or hanging limply. Look to see if a limb drags or is crooked. Look to see if the critter can't stand properly or if one or more of its legs seem paralyzed. Look to see if there is any bleeding from an external wound. Look to see if blood flows from nose or mouth to indicate internal bleeding. Watch to see if your raccoon just lies there or its breathing is rough. Watch for running bowel movements. (Healthy raccoon baby feces on a milk-based diet are formed and yellow in color; weaned, the stool is formed and brown.) Watch for discharge from nose or eyes.

Check for and remove with fingers any external parasites, like fleas, mites, or ticks.

You will need veterinary care to treat any injury or disease. Raccoons can be successfully treated for feline distemper, vaccinated against canine distemper, wormed for the roundworm *Baylisascaris procyonis*. Raccoons with disturbed central nervous system signs may have either canine distemper or rabies—or they may have been hit by a car and have no disease at all.

Zoonoses are diseases that can be passed on from different species to humans. Please check the section on zoonoses in volume seven of this series for further details. Rabies, distemper, and raccoon roundworm are particularly dangerous to humans and no one unqualified should attempt to handle raccoons with these problems.

Call a trained rehabilitator if you know one, or call your Department of Environmental Protection, your vet or local police who will have numbers of a wildlife rehabilitator near you, for help or advice. Do not handle raccoons with disturbed neurological signs (convulsions, paralysis, facial twitching) without help and proper training.

REMEMBER:

DO NOT feed your baby yet. A baby raccoon will react to a change from its mother's milk to your formula. Also, it may be dehydrated. Pinch to tent the skin. If skin is slow to return to normal position (greater than 1-2 seconds), your baby needs more than initial rehydration. Severe dehydration requires a vet's subcutaneous injection.

DO give even a healthy baby a special drink first called a rehydrating solution. Mix:

1 teaspoon salt		1/3 teaspoon salt
3 Tablespoons sugar	or	1 Tablespoon sugar
1 quart warm water		1 cup water

The above is a homemade solution. Commercially available electrolyte solutions such as Pedialyte can also be given or Lactated Ringers solution is available from your veterinarian.

You can offer the drink from a pet nurser or a nipple attached to a syringe for newborns. Use a human baby bottle for bigger kits. Raccoons have a strong sucking habit. Use premie nipples with small openings to prevent aspiration of the formula into the lungs. Offer 4cc's to 8cc's every fifteen minutes for the first hour. Check with your wildlife rehabilitator to find out whether to continue with rehydrating fluid for the first twenty-four to thirty-six hours.

Make certain to keep your baby warm. Make certain to keep it resting quietly in a semi-dark place in between feedings to reduce stress. At this point, do not play with your rehabilitant.

QUIET is the watchword for babies.

IDENTIFICATION AND STAGES OF GROWTH

While your baby raccoon rests, read about its needs, its ways of life in the wild, where it nests, what its food, play, and rest requirements are. A really good wildlife mammal field guide will be in your public library if you don't own one. You need to find out your raccoon's age to feed it the proper diet and house it in the proper way.

Here is a page of raccoons at different ages and stages of development.

Infant: Eyes and ear canals closed at birth, thin layer of fur, facial mask develops at 2 weeks, the tail color rings at 3 weeks. Eyes and ears open after 18 to 24 days.

Juvenile: At 6 weeks, guard hairs appear; crawling and walking begin at 4 to 6 weeks; at 7 weeks, climbing and exploring outside of nest; starting to follow mother and to forage at 8-12 weeks; in the wild, weaning begins before 16 weeks.

Adult: Bushy-tailed; self-feeding; in the wild, weaned by 16 weeks; by late fall may weigh 15 pounds; may winter with mother and siblings; dormant, though not a true hibernation, in winter; yearling female may breed January to March; nocturnal, though may forage in daylight hours.

Different aged raccoons eat differently. Feed your raccoon properly to help it grow properly.

Newborn raccoon

Juvenile raccoons.

3
BASIC DIET

Baby Raccoon Check List

1. You have got your raccoon warm, rested, and calm.

2. You have seen it is not too hurt or stressed.

3. You have given it rehydration fluid.

4. You have identified your raccoon's age in your book and read as well about its natural habitat, natural foods, natural habits. All of this will help you care for it better.

Feed Your Raccoon

You begin by mixing formula. The baby raccoon's formula is closest to a kitten's. KMR is recommended. Before the eyes are open, leave out the cereal and applesauce.

This is the formula we are using currently. You can use the same formula for a nursling badger, black bear, bobcat, mink, otter, skunk, weasel. For nursling fox, feed same formula but use puppy-replacement Esbilac. Mix:

2 parts water

1 part KMR (or use other kitten replacement formula powder and mix according to manufacturer's directions)

1 part baby rice or oatmeal or high-protein cereal

1 part applesauce (pure, no preservatives)

Theralin (vitamin and mineral supplement) (amount according to package directions, powder or liquid)

Nutri-Cal is a high-caloric food supplement. It comes in a tube, tastes good, and helps stimulate appetite. Ask your vet.

Aspirating formula can cause pneumonia. Raccoons suck strongly. Make certain your formula is not too thin by adding cereal or using a nipple with a smaller hole, or a syringe. Wash nipples and syringes thoroughly between feedings, bottles every day. Make enough formula only for a twenty-four hour period. Hold baby upright or on its stomach to feed: never on its back.

Feeding Chart

Birth to one week	4-6cc's every 2 hours (1 time at night)
1-2 weeks	6-8cc's every 2 hours (1 time at night)
2-3 weeks	15-50 cc's every 3 hours
3-4 weeks	50-60cc's every 3-4 hours
4-8 weeks	60cc's every 4 hours

IMPORTANT: Until eyes open, you must stimulate elimination and urination as raccoon mothers do. Gently rub the genital region with moistened cotton ball or tissue. Discontinue stimulation after two minutes whether elimination has occurred or not. You must do this until it becomes obvious babies are eliminating and urinating on their own. For bloat, submerge the lower body in warm water, and massage it for about five minutes. Dry thoroughly. See volume seven of this series for more about bloat.

Never overfeed: tummy should be round and firm as a marshmallow, not tight.

Weaning: At 5-6 weeks, begin to leave solid foods in cage. Offer foods such as moistened puppy kibble, high protein dog food, raw, boned fish, fruits, vegetables, insects, shellfish. By nine weeks, there should be no more bottle feeding. After weaning, offer dry kibble at all times, plus natural foods: grapes, berries, bananas, apples, walnuts, acorns, peanuts, eggs, crayfish, mealworm larvae, anchovies—all are much loved by raccoons. Raccoons , skunks, and foxes are omnivorous (badgers, bobcats, minks, river otters, and weasels are strictly meat-eaters).

Offer a bowl of water at all times. This is not only for drinking, but because raccoons prefer to wash their food before eating it. This has little to do with cleanliness. The water may sensitize their paws to whatever they are eating.

Remember: by 16 to 20 weeks, your raccoon should be ready for release.

Adult

If you have an injured adult, feed 80% balanced commercial ration, 20% of other above foods. Feed 5% of body weight. Feed once a day at dusk.

4
HOUSING

First Home

You have housed your raccoons in a small indoor cage with nest box. At eight weeks, around the time they are weaned, it is time for them to go into an outside caging unit.

Second Home

This has a flight shelf (a shelf or ledge firmly attached 5 to 6 feet above ground) for the nest box to encourage climbing, a sheltered area for bad weather and for the feeling of security. Give your raccoons a stimulating environment. Hammocks, hollow logs, tree trunks with branches for climbing, and a child's swimming pool for water play. Outdoor habitats can be made of 2x3's and wrapped with hardware cloth or chain link, including the flooring so that raccoons can't dig their way out and self-release. A double-door is advisable for the same reason. The size is typically 6'x8'x8' for four to six raccoons. Do not use pressure-treated lumber as it can be toxic.

IMPORTANT: Because of raccoon roundworm which can be lethal to other species, including humans, the floors of raccoon habitats need to be of materials strong enough to allow for thorough cleaning with a blow torch or very strong disinfectants. Dispose of, preferably burn, all raccoon waste.

Again, a word about your domestic animals: Keep them away from your raccoons, not for their sake, but for the sake of your wild creatures. You are not only nurturer, but teacher. You don't want your raccoons approaching other people's pets after release and getting shot. Also, REMEMBER TO VACCINATE YOUR PETS AGAINST RABIES. It's the best protection you and your family has against your pet's bringing home the disease from infected raccoons in the wild.

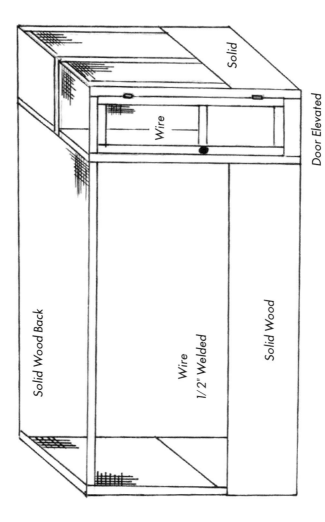

Solid Top

Solid

Door Elevated

Solid Wood Back

Wire
1/2" Welded

Solid Wood

Wire

RACCOON HABITAT

169

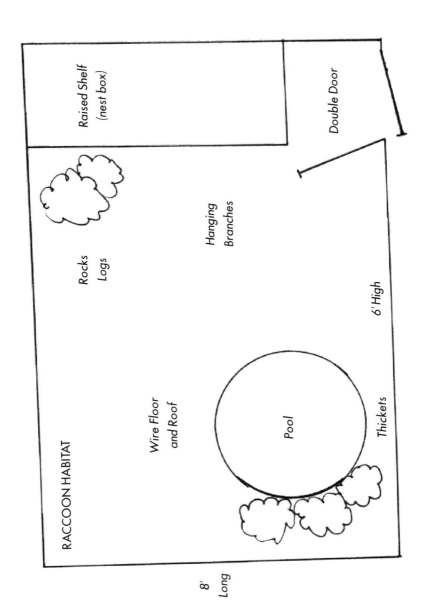

RACCOON HABITAT

Raised Shelf
(nest box)

Double Door

Rocks
Logs

Hanging
Branches

Wire Floor
and Roof

Pool

Thickets

6' High

8'
Long

5
RELEASE

Before you release your raccoons, be sure you have been feeding them at dusk or later. They must be learning to eat at night.

Release your raccoons at about 20 weeks old. You can release a little earlier in a protected area if you want to provide backup food. Otherwise, they must be really self-sufficient, and no longer friendly even to you. Release sites should have water (stream, lake, marsh), woods with logs and trees for climbing and nesting, and they should be as far from human habitats, roads, cars, hunting sites as possible. It is important to check with local natural resource officials to make certain of the carrying capacity of conspecifics (other raccoons), but even more important to discover whether other rehabilitators or biologists are using the site to reestablish raccoon prey species like ground-nesting birds.

Check your weather forecast for three days of good weather. Leave a supply of dry dog food at the base of a tree at least for the first feeding. To capture your raccoons in your own habitat for release, leave a large pet carrier with tempting food, nesting materials from the nest box, inside the larger habitat. If the raccoons do not enter willingly at dawn to nest so that you can close the carrier door, you may have to net them and place them in your carrier.

Release them late in August so they have plenty of time to establish a territory and nest, and put on a fat layer before winter. Release them at dusk. Remember, they are nocturnal. Release them in groups of two or more for company.

Go home happy. You have done well, given your rehabilitants a wonderful start.

We do, of course, accept the limitations of wildlife rehabilitation. Not every animal can be saved. Not all animals will be releasable. The success of released animals cannot be guaranteed. But there are few guarantees in the wild, either.

The point is to do what we can. Wildlife rehabilitators accept, nurture, and release thousands of birds and mammals each year. We train new volunteers. We teach. We learn. You are welcome among us.

6
TIPS

Hot Tips for You

1. Don't handle a raccoon if you don't want to.

2. Call for help and advice.

3. Don't kidnap a baby raccoon. Watch for mother before rescuing.

4. Your goal in rescuing a raccoon is its release when possible. No creature wants a life in prison unless it is too hurt to survive in the wild.

5. If you find an injured adult raccoon, wear gloves.

6. Keep any critter away from your face.

7. Wash hands first for raccoon's sake.

8. Wash hands after handling for your own sake.

Hot Tips for Raccoons

1. In the case of found babies, watch for mother first. DON'T RACCOONNAP while mother is looking for food.

2. Warm raccoon first in your hands, or against your body.

3. Put in warm, quiet place.

4. Generally, it's a good idea to give rehydration solution before food.

5. NEVER FEED a cold, starving raccoon or any other critter before warming and rehydrating.

6. Keep household pets away, however gentle. Raccoons and other small wildlife need to learn to fear cats and dogs.

7. Call Department of Environmental Protection, or your local wildlife rehabilitator, for advice and help. Your veterinarian or local police will have telephone numbers.

I FOUND A BABY SQUIRREL, WHAT DO I DO?

DALE CARLSON
ILLUSTRATED BY HOPE M. DOUGLAS

CONTENTS

1

RESCUE

Why Squirrels Get Hurt

Squirrels get hurt from the impact of falling from nests. They are injured from being attacked by other wild species.

Squirrels get hurt more often from the impact of human beings and our cars, trucks, and bikes, our traps and guns, and even more by our very invasion of their world to cut down their trees and build our own homes to replace theirs.

They are attacked by human companions, dogs and cats.

They get sick from our poisons, caught in our nets.

But whether they are hurt in nature by tree falls and predators, in the country or in city parks, you can learn to help them.

Watch, Wait, Warm

Watch the squirrel that seems stranded on the ground or a low limb for an hour or so first. Often the mother is nearby, watching, chattering to distract you, or even off feeding herself so that she can nurse her young.

Wait until you are sure the baby is abandoned or orphaned. A mother squirrel, unlike a bird, can carry a baby who has simply fallen from the nest back to safety. Our first impulse may be to rush in and rescue, making an orphan out of a baby who was just fine.

A NOTE HERE: once in a while a mother with too large a litter for her to feed—squirrel mothers may have seven or eight kits—may push out a runt or two from the nest. With care, sometimes you can save these.

Normally, however, if a mother doesn't return to look for her young, she has been killed.

Warm the baby. Make a nest of your hands, cupping the baby squirrel to keep it warm, quiet, and in restful darkness. It will be shocked and scared from its fall, or from crawling out of the nest to look for its mother to nurse. Often you will not know whether you have a discarded runt, or a strong, healthy baby crawling out of the nest to look for its mother.

Don't be frightened, as a baby squirrel does not bite. If you're dealing with an injured adult, you'll be wearing heavy-duty leather gloves so that you can pick it up safely.

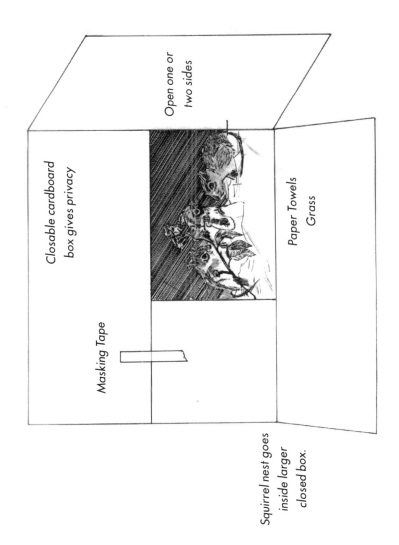

Closable cardboard
box gives privacy

Open one or
two sides

Masking Tape

Paper Towels

Grass

Squirrel nest goes
inside larger
closed box.

Once you are certain the baby is orphaned or abandoned, carry the squirrel gently in your hands. If you find several squirrels, or you are dealing with an adult, you cannot simply cup your hands. You will need a small box with a cover. Line it with soft cloth or paper toweling. Be sure there are breathing holes in the box.

You will need the help of a licensed rehabilitator to care for the baby. This is true even if you are a practiced rehabilitator of other species but without experience with squirrels. This is true even more if the squirrel is injured or has symptoms of dehydration or illness.

DO continue to keep the squirrel warm.

DO NOT feed it food or water right away as this could distress or harm a cold, shocked creature.

Initial Care

Place your squirrel, or squirrels, in a warm, quiet, semi-dark place. You will need two boxes: a small box for a nest, and a larger one to put the nest box inside of.

Make the nest box out of a small wooden or cardboard box, with the opening at one side. It is important for the squirrel baby to have a private place to crawl in and out of. To begin with, a ski cap is a perfect, warming place inside the larger container. Always keep the baby in a small nest inside the larger box for warmth and privacy.

And always keep it warm. Provide continued warmth with a heating pad set on low underneath (not in) 1/3 of the outside container.

At first a cardboard box will do for the larger container. An aquarium with a wire net cover is fine. Line it with paper toweling, or an old T-shirt or clean flannel cloth or piece of sheet. Never use colored newspaper (poison) nor shredding towels (to catch nails or choke in).

Later, when a larger space is necessary, put the nest box inside a dog crate wrapped in the stiff wire of 1/2" hardware cloth. This will keep your baby in, and your pets or other species of visitors out.

Put your baby inside the smaller nest box and the nest box inside the larger container. Also add leaves and grass for your squirrel to use as nesting material, small tree branches to climb, bark to chew, twigs to sharpen teeth on, pine cones to play with. Housing needs will change from birth to release, from aquarium size containers to outdoor habitats 6'L x 4'W x 6'H for prerelease juveniles and adults.

Continue to keep the baby warm, but never hot! Remember to keep the heating pad set low outside the outer box.

Watch now, don't handle for a while. After an hour of rest, unless your baby squirrel has another squirrel for company, it will be lonely. Gentle but not constant cuddling is good for baby squirrels. But best of all, find it another orphaned squirrel (call another rehabilitator) to grow up with. Squirrels need their own kind for company and for socializing skills.

First Aid

You will need to do a basic physical examination to see if your squirrel is hurt. Watch it to see if it seems hurt. Look to see if the limbs are placed properly in relationship to the body, not bent or twisted or hanging limply. Look to see if a limb drags or is bent and held up against the body for too long or is crooked. Look to see if it can't stand properly or one of its hind legs or both seem paralyzed. (There is a disease that can paralyze squirrels, or there may be a spinal cord injury). Look to see if there is any bleeding from an external wound. Look to see if blood flows from nose or mouth to indicate internal bleeding. Watch to see if the squirrel just lies there or if the breathing is rough. Watch for running bowel movements. (Healthy squirrel bowel movements are little brown pellets.) Watch for discharge from nose or eyes. See volume seven of this series.

As you make your examination, pick off any external parasites, fleas, mites, or ticks, with your fingernails or carefully with a tweezer.

Begin to make a record of where and when you found or acquired it and its general condition.

You will need help to treat any injury or disease. Squirrels can suffer from several health problems such as mange, abscesses, viruses, and bacteria that affect respiratory and digestive systems, and central nervous system disorders resulting from raccoon roundworm infections. Your squirrel may also have head/spinal cord injuries.

Call for advice. Call a trained animal rehabilitator if you know one. If not, call your Department of Environmental Protection, or your veterinarian, or local police, who will have telephone numbers for a wildlife rehabilitator near you.

REMEMBER:

DO NOT feed it immediately. A baby squirrel may eat too fast and aspirate (fill its lungs and drown) if it is too hungry.

DO give it a special drink first called a rehydrating solution. Mix:

1 teaspoon salt		1/3 teaspoon salt
3 Tablespoons sugar	or	1 Tablespoon sugar
1 quart warm water		1 cup warm water

The above is a homemade solution. Commercially available electrolyte solutions such as Pedialyte (available at supermarkets in baby food section) can also be given, as well as Lactated Ringers solution. There is also Amino Acid Solution (ask your vet or local pet store) to use as a transitional rehydrating formula from intake to the point when the infant can properly digest the concentrated replacement formula.

You can offer the drink in a small plastic dropper, or from the long-shaped nipple of a pet nurser bottle attached either to bottle or syringe. Offer 4cc's to 8cc's every two or three hours slowly for the first twenty-four hours.

Let your squirrel rest quietly in between rehydration feedings.

For a squirrel whose eyes are open, offer grape halves, bits of watermelon, berries to rehydrate, restore body fluids, and nourish.

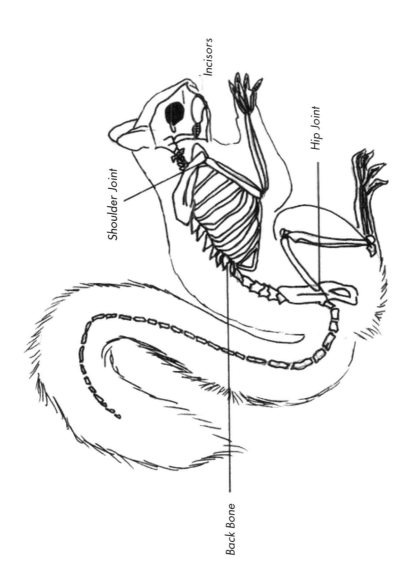

Incisors

Hip Joint

Shoulder Joint

Back Bone

189

2
IDENTIFICATION AND STAGES OF GROWTH

You will need to know what kind of squirrel you have for eventual proper diet and housing. Look at your squirrel again carefully, for size, amount of fur, markings, whether the eyes are open or closed. Then look at a really good wildlife field guide mammal book. You can find wildlife books in your public library if you don't own one. Add the information you find to the record you have begun to keep: the date and circumstances of your acquiring the squirrel, your examination, your initial care. All this will help you in your rehabilitation, and to answer questions asked by veterinarians and other rehabilitators.

Here is a page of some common squirrels.

1. Tree squirrels: Eastern gray squirrel, Western gray squirrel, Southern flying squirrel, Eastern fox squirrel

2. Ground squirrels and prairie dogs: California ground squirrel, spotted ground squirrel, Blacktail prairie dog

3. Striped squirrels: Red squirrel, Eastern chipmunk, Chickaree

Diet, habitat, markings, and habits divide squirrels into four categories: tree squirrels; flying squirrels; ground squirrels; and chipmunks.

KAIBAB SQUIRREL
18¼ - 23"

WESTERN
GRAY 20½ - 22⅜"

FOX SQUIRREL
17½ - 27½"

RED SQUIRREL
10½ - 15¼"

GRAY SQUIRREL
16⅞ - 19¾"

NORTHERN FLYING
SQUIRREL 10¾ - 14½"

SOUTHERN FLYING
SQUIRREL 8¼ - 10"

You need to know a squirrel's age to feed and house it properly. Here are squirrels at different ages and stages of development.

Infant: eyes and ears closed, pink and hairless for the first week; at two weeks skin darkens; and by three weeks hair is noticeable

Juvenile: ears and eyes open (4-5 weeks), furred, tail sparse; by five weeks eyes are focusing, body is about 10", tail 41/2", baby more active, still needs formula, but may begin nibbling solids

Adult: bushy-tailed, self-feeding (age weaned in wild, 8-12 weeks, not self-supporting until 12 weeks old) eats solid, natural foods, explores outside nest, learns to crack nuts, releasable from captivity 12-14 weeks of age

Different aged squirrels eat differently. The wrong food fed wrongly will not help your squirrel to grow properly and thrive.

Infant Squirrels

Juvenile Squirrels.

Adult Squirrel

3
BASIC DIET

Baby Squirrel Checklist

1. You have got your squirrel warm, rested, and calm.

2. You have seen it is not too hurt or stressed.

3. You have given it rehydration fluid.

4. You have identified your squirrel as to whether you have a bushy-tailed tree squirrel, a flying squirrel, a ground squirrel, or chipmunk, and its age in your field guide. You have read as well about its natural habitat, natural foods, natural habits. You have numbers of wildlife rehabilitation centers and organizations to call for correct diet and feeding techniques.

Feed Your Squirrel

You begin by mixing formula, just as you would for any baby mammal. The infant squirrel's formula we call BMF, Basic Mammal Formula. It can be given to most baby mammals such as woodchucks and skunks as well, in our experience. Before the eyes open, the nutritional requirements of most young mammals can be met by a puppy or kitten replacement (not cow milk!) liquid or powder mix formula. After the eyes are open, and checking on the look of the bowel movement, use BMF. For your baby squirrel mix:

2 parts water

1 part Esbilac (or use other puppy replacement formula powder such as Unilac and mix according to manufacturer's directions)

1 part baby rice or oatmeal or high-protein cereal

1 part applesauce (pure, no preservatives or extra sugar)

Theralin (puppy replacement vitamin and mineral supplement, amount according to package directions, powder or liquid)

Nutri-Cal is a high caloric, dietary supplement your veterinarian can give you for runty young or for those who do not seem to be eating enough. It comes in a tube, tastes good, and may stimulate appetite.

For infant squirrels whose eyes are still closed, the simple formula diet is best. Do not make it so thin your baby squirrel aspirates (sucks the liquid into its lungs, which causes a pneumonia-like condition that can kill). Also, to prevent aspiration, use a nipple with a smaller hole, or, if you need more control over the flow, a syringe with or without nipple, or a plastic dropper.

For larger infants and juveniles, thicken the formula with more cereal and applesauce.

Some young will suck strongly. Others may lap. Wash nipples and syringes thoroughly between feedings, bottles every day. Make enough formula only for a twenty-four-hour period.

Feeding Chart

Birth to one week	1cc to 2cc every 2 hours (even through night)
1-2 weeks	2cc to 4cc every 2 hours (4 hour break night)
2-3 weeks	4cc to 6cc every 3 hours
3-4 weeks	8cc to 10cc every 3 hours
4-6 weeks	10cc to 15cc every 4 hours
6-8 weeks	15cc to 18cc 3-4x per day

IMPORTANT: Until eyes open, you must stimulate elimination and urination as squirrel mothers do. Gently rub the genital region with moistened cotton ball or tissue. You must do this until it becomes obvious they are eliminating on their own. There is a reason for this need: mothers squirrels remove their young from the nest and stimulate their elimination outside it in order not to attract predators by nest odors.

While the squirrels are on formula, their stools will be mustard color and the consistency of toothpaste. Off the formula, normal droppings are tiny brown pellets.

Solids: As eyes open, introduce solid foods. Bird food with nuts, fruits, and sunflower seeds (we use parrot mix), berries, apple bits, grapes, watermelon with seeds, peanuts (raw, no salt, please), and all other nuts, especially cracked walnuts, acorns, filberts, beech nuts, elm and oak flowers and buds, pine cones, carrots, corn on cob, broccoli. Dog or cat kibble is a good transitional food. Rodent lab chow pellets (never rabbit chow) is an excellent supplement. In preparation for release, offer nuts and seeds most often found in area. Always keep a small bowl of fresh water available. Begin to wean from the bottle at 8 or 9 weeks. At 12-14 weeks, your squirrels should be self-feeding and ready for release.

4
HOUSING

First Home

You have already made a small nest box inside a larger container, aquarium, or hardware-clothed dog crate, for your squirrel. And because baby squirrels cannot yet thermoregulate (keep their body temperatures regulated) you have kept a heating pad under the container or cage set on low around the clock until eyes open. As your squirrels open their eyes, this container may be put outside during the day (well-protected from pets and predators) if it is warm weather, and kept indoors if it is cold.

Second Home

If the container or aquarium is small, squirrels should now be kept in the larger, hardware-clothed dog crate. They will let you know when it is time for larger quarters as they begin to do the Indy 500 around their present quarters. You have added sturdy climbing branches for playing, eating, and hiding, grass for nesting, pine cones, bark and twigs for chewing.

Increase the size of the cage as necessary, making sure to transfer the nest box with its familiar bit of nest cloth from the first days. Again, this cage may be outdoors in warm weather, but should be protected indoors if it is cold.

You have added a constant supply of solid foods, fruits and vegetables, nuts and cones, and a dish of water or lab water bottle kept fresh.

Third Home

As the animal needs more exercise, and in preparation for release so that it adjusts to outside temperatures and smells, you should house your squirrels outside in a habitat 6' by 6', a structure entirely, including the ground flooring, wrapped (like a Christmas present) in 1/2" hardware cloth just like your indoor dog crate or cage. This prevents premature self-releasing. It also prevents raccoons or other predators from tunneling in. Rats, often attracted to rehabilitants' water and feed, can chew their way into habitats unless these are well-protected or you are willing to control rat population.

You will need a high shelf for the nest box. Or you can tie a crate lined with grass or leaves toward the upper portion of the larger habitat. As before, transfer some of the original nesting material. Naturalize the habitat with larger branches, logs, grass, to accustom the squirrels to their natural woodland environment.

A word about your domestic animals once more: you are not only nurturer, but teacher. Your squirrels must learn to be shy of your pets, and you, and all other natural predators.

Companionship

I use the plural because it is important to raise squirrels in groups and not alone so that they develop normal socialization skills. Squirrels are social animals. A single will attach itself to you and may approach the wrong person later on if it is hungry out in the wild. Squirrels brought up together teach one another and mature more naturally. Also, when release time comes, they will have company instead of being alone out there.

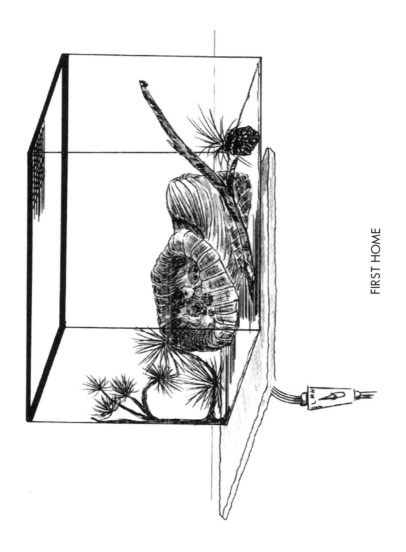

FIRST HOME

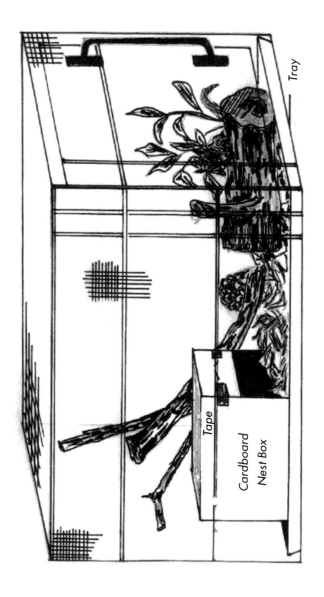

Tray

Tape

Cardboard Nest Box

SECOND HOME
Dog crate covered with hardware cloth

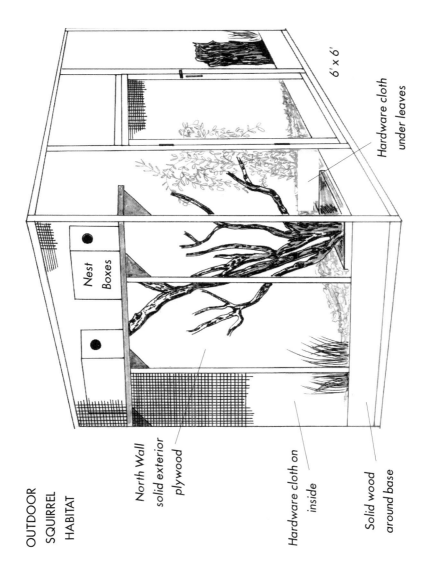

OUTDOOR
SQUIRREL
HABITAT

North Wall
solid exterior
plywood

Nest
Boxes

Hardware cloth on
inside

Solid wood
around base

6' x 6'

Hardware cloth
under leaves

At 12-14 weeks, your squirrels are ready for release.

They are bushy-tailed.

They are self-feeding. The nuts you once cracked for them, they can now crack by themselves, acorns certainly, even walnuts.

You have not habituated them to (gotten them used to) you or your household pets.

They are thermoregulated—used to outdoor temperatures.

They are going crazy in captivity.

Your squirrels have wild genes. You have taught them all they need to live free. It is time for letting go.

You will have talked to local natural resource officials, other wildlife rehabilitators, about appropriate release sites—where there are other similar squirrels but not an overload, where there are not too many natural predators like raccoons and hawks, and above all, where there are not too many human beings with their cars and pets.

Transfer Technique

One of the trickier aspects of caring for wildlife is the release technique. At release time, your animals have already wilded up. You can no longer just take them in your hand and tuck them into a carrier.

You can leave a pet carrier in their habitat. Remove their nest, so that at night the only place for them to go is into the pet carrier. This must be on the flight shelf or tied high, as your squirrels know better than to sleep on the ground. Transfer their nesting material into the carrier. A second method is simply to wait until they are sleeping in their nest box, cover this with a large cloth, and transfer the nest box into a carrier.

In the morning, you can carry them deep into the safety of the woods far away from human habitation.

Or you can do a soft release if you live near an appropriate environment. Put the old, indoor crate on top of the outdoor environment. Take off the hardware cloth so that the squirrels can get in but raccoons cannot reach in and prey on them as they sleep. Put the nest box for protection inside the crate with food in it or near it. Make certain the crate door is closed. Your squirrels will come and go as they please until they are ready to either run away forever, or take up residence right in your own trees in your own back yard.

They need to be released early in the day when good weather is promised for three days, warm, no storms.

They need to be released early enough before winter to store away food. They need to live among nut and fruiting trees to find more food.

It is up to you to decide on the best environment for them.

The release is the most important part after nurturing wildlife, remembering always they are not ours to keep, but to help in their distress and to let go.

Your squirrels may grow strong and when released run right up a tree and out of your life into a life of their own. But there are some who do not or cannot thrive. Sometimes, they hurt too much and die. Sometimes there are developmental problems, and they cannot thrive. These things are not your fault. You can only protect a squirrel's life and its dying, keep it fed, warmed, and safe from fear and predators.

Grief over release or death is a normal part of rehabilitating. We have always found a rehabilitator's relief from grief is simply to help the next creature in distress.

6
TIPS

Hot Tips for You

1. Don't handle a squirrel if you don't want to.

2. Call for help and advice.

3. Don't critternap a baby squirrel. Watch for mother before rescuing.

4. Your goal in rescuing a squirrel is its release when possible. No critter wants a life prison sentence unless it is too hurt to survive in the wild.

5. Wear gloves for adult squirrels. They bite.

6. Keep any critter away from your face.

7. Wash hands first for squirrel's sake.

8. Wash hands after handling for your own sake.

Hot Tips for Critters

1. In the case of found babies, watch for parents first: DON'T CRITTERNAP while mother is off to find food.

2. Warm baby squirrel first in your hands, or against your body. A wounded adult must be handled with gloves, placed in a covered box, transported to a cage, and, if cold, placed in the container over an exterior heating pad set on low.

3. Put in warm, quiet, dark place to recover from shock.

4. Generally, it is a good idea to give rehydration solution before food.

5. NEVER FEED a cold, starving critter before warming and rehydrating.

6. Keep household pets away, however gentle. Squirrels and other small wildlife need to learn to fear cats and dogs.

7. Call your Department of Environmental Protection, or your local wildlife rehabilitator, for advice and help. Your veterinarian or your local police have telephone numbers.

FIRST AID FOR WILDLIFE
BASIC CARE FOR BIRDS AND MAMMALS

IRENE RUTH
ILLUSTRATED BY HOPE DOUGLAS, M.A.

CONTENTS

1
THE RESCUE AND RESCUE KIT

Your reaction to an injured or trapped creature will be almost instinctive; you will want to relieve the animal of its distress immediately. But think before you act. Use your head before your heart's reaction. You need to assess the situation and then decide whether you will—or can—assist this animal.

EVALUATION
Each situation will be different and must be evaluated. Ask these questions.

- What kind of animal is this?

- Is it an adult or a juvenile?

- What is its situation?

- Does it actually need your help?

- Is it possible for you to help it?

- Is it safe for you to help it?

A few minutes now can save both you and the animal trouble later on. Animals have defenses. Remember these, and treat their defenses with respect and understanding. Their defenses aren't much against our guns.

Safety for the Animal

- Do not critternap—a fledgling may only be learning to fly; fawn and rabbit babies are often left alone for hours while mothers feed

- Watch and wait at least 4 hours for rabbits and fawns; at least 2 hours for raccoon mothers to return: call a rehabilitator for advice

Safety for You

- Never handle a bird alone too large to manage easily

- Watch for beaks and claws; do not handle raptors such as hawks and eagles by yourself (call for professional help)

- Rabies species, including raccoons, skunks, foxes, bats, **are not** necessarily sick if out in daytime and may just be hungry: to determine illness, watch for central nervous system symptoms (convulsions, facial spasms, paralysis, staggering) and remember that these may also be due to a car hit or distemper

GUIDELINES

Here are a few guidelines to help you decide if an animal needs to be rescued.

Help a bird if:

- There is blood, an open wound, or a recognizable break

- It cannot stand on its own

- One of its legs is hanging useless

- It cannot fly and is not a nestling or fledgling being coached by nearby parents (always watch and wait to make certain it is orphaned)

- The beak is damaged

- It has oil on its feathers

- It is definitely caught in a trap

- You recognize it as an exotic species (these cannot fend for themselves)

- It is a bird of prey or swan having only one foot or leg, or there is a fishing line or string caught on the bird

- The bird has been caught by a cat even if it seems fine

- The bird is unconscious

- If there is any difficulty breathing

Leave the bird alone if:

- You are not absolutely certain it is orphaned

- It is a swan grazing in a field

- It is standing on one leg

- It is any bird with only one eye except hawks

- You would endanger yourself and others

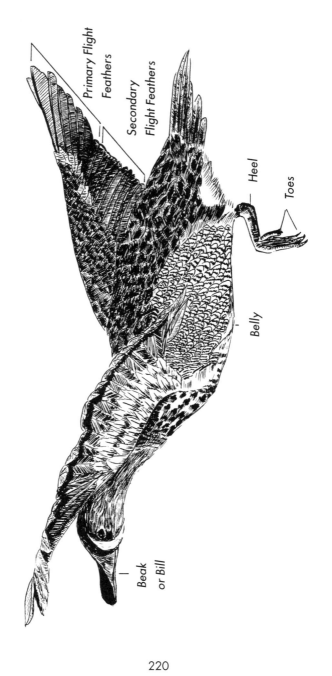

Primary Flight Feathers

Secondary Flight Feathers

Heel

Toes

Belly

Beak or Bill

220

Help a mammal if:

- You can see open wounds or other injuries

- It has been hit by a car

- A leg appears damaged

- It is dragging two legs

- It is caught in a fence or trap

- It has been attacked by a predator

- It has been caught by a cat, even if it seems fine

- It is an orphan not ready to be on its own (you wait and watch to see if the mother is simply away foraging for food, or the nest is destroyed and the mother waiting until you leave to move her babies)

- The animal is unconscious

- It is having trouble breathing

Leave a mammal alone if:

- It is a normally nocturnal animal out during the day (it may be just hungry or a nursing mother looking for extra food)

- You are not absolutely certain an infant or juvenile is an orphan

- The animal is too big or too dangerous for you to handle safely (any hurt animal may bite or become aggressive), call your Department of Environmental Protection or U.S. Fish and Wildlife Department, or the local police—have numbers handy

Animals love their young

- It is showing possible signs of rabies (lack of coordination, circling, unprovoked aggressiveness, drooling, convulsing, facial tics, paralysis, or extreme tameness): if these signs are present, notify the police or animal control officer, and do not touch the animal or allow other humans and animals to approach

IMMEDIATE AID

If you have decided that the animal needs your care, be calm and deliberate. A deep breath helps. You will make fewer mistakes, and the animal will react positively to your calm.

First make sure that you have everything you are going to need. You can't put a rescue on hold while you go get something you have forgotten. Carry some simple items in your car and your work can begin right away.

ITEMS FOR YOUR CAR

- a strong, covered, ventilated container, heavy cardboard or plastic (this protects you and comforts and contains the animal)

- blanket, towels

- thick gloves for your protection

- a lightweight shovel (often better than hands for lifting an injured animal into container or to the side of the road—an injured creature may bite or carry parasites)

- wire cutters and scissors for traps, fences, fishing line, and so forth

THE CAPTURE

Be calm, and move quietly and smoothly. Make all of your actions firm but gentle. Quiet talk seems to reassure some animals, but watch for reactions and stop if it seems to upset.

Avoid looking directly into an animal's eyes, as a direct gaze is sometimes seen as threatening. Remember we are a predator species; they are right to fear us.

Your own protection should be your top priority. If you are injured helping this animal, who will be available to help the others?

Wear gloves, heavy ones like welding gloves, for picking up mammals and the large birds, rubber gloves for smaller birds and infants. Keep your face out of the animal's reach and protect your eyes.

Don't put yourself in danger by climbing high trees, going near powerlines, trying to work in pitch dark, going into traffic.

You will have better luck with your capture if you guide or lure rather than chase an animal into confinement. Herding into a corner situation such as a building, fence, or wall will give you an advantage during capture, but keep in mind that the animal is now cornered, will feel threatened, and may attack.

Approach with caution, but be purposeful. Anticipate a struggle. A humane trap for an adult animal or a possibly rabid one is the best and safest rescue. Keep physical contact to a minimum for your safety and the animal's well-being. Trap and transport. Wear heavy gloves when handling trap. Cover the small bird or mammal with a blanket or towel, your own coat. If it can't see, it will be less apt to struggle. Bring the blanket under and around the animal, trapping wings against the body on birds, and keeping paws and claws covered in mammals.

Put into the transport box and secure immediately. Be as quiet as possible during the capture.

Use only as much restraint as needed, but never underestimate your patient. A terrified animal is stronger than usual.

All creatures have a fight or flight response to danger. Be ready for either.

SITUATIONS

The following are situations in which an animal may be injured or need help.

1. **Car Hits.** Animals that are slow are often hit by cars and trucks. Squirrels are fast, but are hit often because they can't seem to make up their minds which way is safe to go. Crows and hawks are often hit eating roadkill, and owls are hit while chasing small mammals. If you can, without endangering your own life, stop to rescue a wounded animal. If you can, stop to shovel-carry a roadkill to the side of the road, and you will save the life of a hungry animal.

2. **Traps and Snares.** Leg hold traps cause terrible damage to a bird or mammal. Even humane traps like the Havahart traps can be dangerous to an animal who panics and tries to fight its way out or one who has been left in the trap too long without food or water. A bird or mammal may be trapped in a house or office building, a chimney, drainage pipes, barrels, fences, barbed wire, fishing line, garden or sports netting. They may need help because of dehydration or starvation, because of injuries from whatever they were trapped in, or because of injuries sustained while trying to escape. There are animals who will chew at their own legs to escape.

225

3. **Gunshot Wounds.** Hunters, and people "defending" their property against wildlife can wound an animal. Sometimes animals are shot in acts of cruelty and abuse. The animal may escape, but eventually the wound, loss of blood, infection, or stress will take its toll and the animal will need help.

4. **Predator Attack**. All wildlife has natural predators and may sustain tooth and claw injuries from other animals. Humans are predators too, and can intentionally or accidentally cause injuries to wild animals.

5. **Window Hits.** Birds are often injured by flying into windows. They see scenery reflections, not glass.

6. **Glass, Wire, Sharp Metal, Sharp Sticks, Rocks** are all a threat to wild animals.

7. **Fires** in woods or forest areas.

8. **Falls and Slips.** Just living its own life, an animal can be prey to falls and slips from trees, cliffs, slippery rocks, into pools, lakes, ponds, rivers.

9. **Food or Water Shortage.** A bad winter takes its toll, a drought.

10. **Extreme Weather Conditions.**

11. **Oil Spills, Tar, Chemicals** used in swimming pools, on lawns, in cars.

12. **Careless Litter** such as the uncut holes of six-pack plastic, balloons, and fishing lines that can choke, be swallowed, or tangle legs and beaks to cause drowning or starvation.

13. **Lawn Mowers** run over nests of rabbits, moles, shrews, and other small ones.

14. **Diseases and Parasites.**

Try to find out as much as possible about the situation that caused an emergency for the animal. This information can be an important tool in your rescue, in the first aid treatment, and for the professional.

Just a duck

2
HOME AND FIRST AID SUPPLIES

You now have the animal secured in its box, away from outside dangers, and you are ready to begin to help. Try to get the animal to a veterinarian who works with wild animals, or to a wildlife rehabilitator who has experience working with orphaned or injured wildlife. Check with veterinarians in your area to see if they are willing to help. Call your local wildlife department or police to find the names and telephone numbers of rehabilitators near you. Keep these numbers available.

If you can reach someone to help you right away, your work is done. Unfortunately, it is not always possible to reach someone right away. In the meantime, you will want to make the critter as comfortable as possible. You may not be able to fix the injuries or cure the illnesses, but you can stabilize the animals and keep them alive until you can get some professional help.

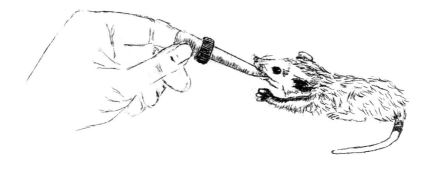

HOME FIRST AID KIT

These items compose a useful home first aid kit for emergency situations.

- a suitable cage or container, cardboard box, plastic box (make sure there are air holes)

- Betadine, Clinidine, Nolvasan, or similar antiseptic wash (do not use hydrogen peroxide as it spreads bacteria into healthy tissue)

- triple antibiotic ointment, germicidal soap, petroleum jelly

- a dehydrating solution such as Pedialyte (any supermarket in baby section), Lactated Ringers (veterinarian supply), or you can make your own with:

  1 quart warm water   1 cup warm water

  3 Tablespoons sugar   3/4 Tablespoon sugar

  1 teaspoon salt   1/4 teaspoon salt

- Kaopectate or Pepto Bismol

- flea and tick water-based (safe for kittens) liquid spray containing pyrethrins (powders can be inhaled and damage eyes of birds and small mammals)

- syringes, eyedropper

- tweezers

- bandages, gauze and cotton, and tape, adhesive, masking or nonstick

- towels, soft cloths, blankets (no ragged edges, loops, holes)

- paper towels

- rubber gloves

- heavy, protective gloves, like fireplace or welders gloves

- can of puppy or kitten milk replacer, applesauce, baby rice cereal

3

PROBLEM CHECKLIST AND THE PHYSICAL EXAMINATION

PROBLEM CHECKLIST

There is a moment of fear when you first hold a distressed creature. You do not know what is wrong. You are not certain you can deal with the injury or illness. You doubt your knowledge and capacities. It will help to go over this general checklist in your mind, to answer your own questions and those of the professional you call and to whom you will take this animal.

Major Categories of Problems in Distressed Animals

- I. Shock

- II. Dehydration

- III. Unconsciousness

- IV. Wounds (injuries involving breaks in the skin)

- V. Fractures
   - A. Simple—no bones protruding
   - B. Compound—bone ends protruding through skin

- VI. Poisoning

- VII. Malnutrition and Starvation

VIII.   Diseases and Infections
  A. Virus
  B. Bacteria
  C. Parasites, external, internal
  D. Zoonotic—diseases that affect humans

IX.   Burns and Scalds

X.   Hypothermia and Hyperthermia

Systems That Can Be Affected

Respiratory	Skeletal	Skin
Nervous	Digestive	Eye and Ear
Muscular		Blood

Some Causes of Problems

- Inherited or Birth Condition
- Transmitted (from another animal)
- Accidents
- Abuse
- Predator Attack
- Parasites
- Infection
- Runtiness

Think about possible causes, symptoms, and then the appropriate treatment.

Preparation

Treat any animal you work with for shock. Once you get it home, place it in a container in a warm, dark, quiet place. Cover the cage or box to reduce visual stress. This is a time for the animal to rest and recover a bit from the stress of the capture and transportation. It is also a time for you to be doing the first part of your physical exam of the mammal or bird...observe. Learn as much as you can before you even begin the hands on part of the exam. This includes watching the animal and referring to your books, both the general reference guides on the creature in its natural habitat so you understand its normal conditions, and any manuals you have on rehabilitation.

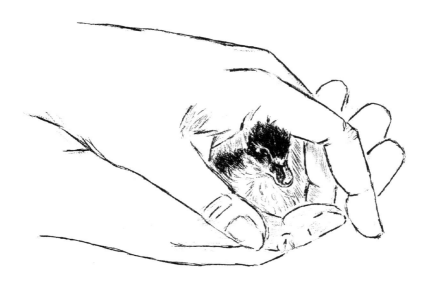

Holding and warming a small one

While the animal rests and you observe, get your supplies ready. Have at hand anything you might possibly need during the exam.

Prepare a gentle surface for the animal to rest on during the exam: toweling, layers of soft cloth, an old sweatshirt.

Have extra soft cloths, bandages, and an antiseptic solution like Betadine ready.

Be prepared for maggots (these look like tiny white worms and are usually very active) in any wound. Remember that these can be a helpful cleansing agent, but do not leave them. You will need to rinse repeatedly with saline solution or other antiseptic rinse, which will cause them to begin to move out of the wound. Use tweezers to remove any that do not rinse out.

Have a plan for examination that you follow consistently with every animal or bird. Start the exam with the head, not forgetting the mouth, and work toward the tail. Or do it in the reverse. The order does not matter, but be consistent and there will be less chance of forgetting something during the actual exam. If you find something wrong, don't stop there. It might not be the only problem. Check everything. A bird with an obvious broken leg may also be choking on an object in its throat.

Wash your hands before and after handling any animal. Wear gloves.

Remember: any injured juvenile or adult can add teeth and agility to its fear of you. It will try to escape. It may claw or bite. It will not enjoy the exam. Be prepared.

While you are doing the exam, look for any signs of ticks and fleas.

Some stress is inevitable during an exam. But if at any time during the exam the animal becomes too stressed (begins to breathe too heavily, struggles enough to hurt itself or you, screams in terror or pain) stop the exam and allow the creature dark and quiet, and then begin again. Too much stress can kill an animal.

Always be on the alert for wounds, punctures, cuts. If you find any, be sure to check for maggots, or maggot eggs, which are beige and look like flakes of oatmeal.

THE EXAMINATION

Head

Are there wounds? Are the eyes bright or sunken? Are they runny? Swollen? Crusty? Closed or opened? Do they respond to light or touch? Are there any maggots, or other foreign objects? A rapid vibration of the eyes may be an indication of concussion.

Check inside the mouth, being very careful. Note the color of the gums. Pale or white gums can mean internal bleeding or anemia. Are the teeth all right? Is there foreign matter like dirt in the mouth? Is there an object in the throat? Is there bleeding from the mouth? Is there beak or jaw damage?

Are the ears clean? Is there bleeding? Are there mites, ticks? Is there a discharge?

Is the neck all right? Does the head wobble? (If the creature is a baby bird, this is normal. Otherwise, it isn't.) Is there head twitch or tilt? Are there wounds?

Limbs

Are there breaks or fractures? Sometimes these are obvious, sometimes you need to compare the right and left limbs to see if there is an abnormality in one by feeling gently along the limbs and into shoulder and hip. Are there breaks in the skin, swelling, misalignments? Are the feet all right?

Body

Are the feathers or fur in good condition? Are they dull, scruffy? Do you see oil or other substances on them?

Feel the chest and abdomen areas, checking for wounds. A sharp, thin keel in birds indicates starvation.

Check the behind to see if there are signs of diarrhea, constipation, prolapsed rectum, worms.

Skin should be loose and pliable, and in mammals provides a good test for dehydration. It should flatten in less than two seconds if pinched into a tent. If the skin is slow to flatten, dehydration is present. The best place to pinch is between the shoulders. For a bird, pinching skin to test for dehydration is unreliable. In birds, dehydration is signaled by apathy, sharp keel (the bird is too thin), slitted and sunken eyes, and a hunched look of misery.

Are there any odors besides the animal's natural odor? Many people, even without training, can detect a sickish odor on an animal in trouble as they can on their own children. Wounds that are infected have a strong odor.

Weigh the animal if it is possible to do so.

Make notes during the examination if you have some help, after the exam if you are working alone. Write down anything you noted during the exam. All of this information will help the veterinarian or rehabilitator later on. Record the critter's weight if you can. This will be important in deciding dosages of medications.

Now make the animal comfortable, and begin to deal with the conditions that you have found.

4
EMERGENCY SITUATIONS AND TREATMENT

No treatment should begin on an animal until the animal has been treated for shock by warming, and kept in a dark, quiet place for at least half an hour. You will know if it is warm enough if it feels warm to the touch.

1. Shock

Symptoms: Drop in body temperature, body feels cold to the touch, a fast but weak pulse, fast, shallow breathing. Lips, gums, tongue, and eye membranes may be pale (this could also indicate internal bleeding). There may also be vomiting, loss of control of urine and bowels, general weakness, and perhaps unconsciousness. Shock reactions in birds can be delayed, sometimes as long as a couple of days. The bird will be weak, listless, have pale membranes.

Causes: Extreme stress, physical or emotional.

Treatment: Keep the shocked animal in a dark, warm, quiet place. Cover the cage or container to reduce visual stress. The animal should have some time of complete isolation.

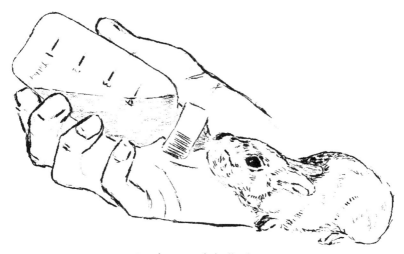

Feed mammals belly down

2. Dehydration or Excessive Loss of Fluids

Symptoms: Sunken eyes, overall shrunken appearance, loss of skin elasticity, non-responsiveness.

Causes: Extreme heat, no available water, prolonged or severe diarrhea.

Treatment: Treat by restoring body fluids. Use Pedialyte, Lactated Ringers solution, or a homemade rehydration solution (1 quart of warm water, 3 Tablespoons of sugar, and one teaspoon of salt, mixed well) to balance the animal's electrolytes. Give this solution by mouth several times within the first hour. For a small mammal, you can use a pet nurser with a nipple, a syringe with a nipple, eye dropper. For larger mammals, an ordinary baby's bottle will do or a large syringe. For birds, the fluid must be dropped onto the beak and allowed to dribble into the mouth. Do not put fluids directly into a bird's mouth, or you risk drowning it by getting fluids into its breathing hole. Alternately, feed small bits of watermelon, berries, or grapes instead of the fluids. When the animal or bird seems more alert and responsive, other food may be introduced slowly. A severely dehydrated animal will need intravenous fluids or subcutaneous fluid injections or drips. This must be done by a qualified professional.

3.   **Unconsciousness**

Symptoms: Little or no response to stimuli.

Causes: Concussion, hypothermia, heat stroke, suffocation, drowning, heart attack, electrocution, and shock can all cause various degrees of unconsciousness.

Treatment: Concussion or stunning is usually caused by a blow to the head, and is temporary. The animal will recover on its own if treated as for shock with a safe, warm, quiet, dark place to rest.

A more serious injury will make the animal unconscious longer. The animal may have trouble with balance or paralysis, and possibly blindness. The animal needs to be checked out by a veterinarian, and possibly treated with steroids to lessen damage from tissue swelling.

Coma is deep unconsciousness, and there will be no reflexes evident at all. This can result from severe brain injury, poisoning, or high temperatures. This condition also needs veterinary care.

4. Open Wounds and Bleeding

Symptoms: Blood, visible tears in the flesh.

Causes and Types:

a. incisions—caused by sharp, tearing objects like glass or metal

b. punctures and closed wounds—caused by sharp, pointy objects like nails, teeth, sharp sticks, thorns, and by bullets or pellets (especially dangerous as the flesh may seal over them and they can become infected easily; punctures may also be much deeper than they appear)

c. lacerations—torn flesh usually with jagged edges (these require veterinary attention)

d. bruises and scrapes can be caused by skidding on a hard surface, by kicks or blows from a stick or club—there may not be much bleeding involved superficially

Treatment: To stop severe bleeding, apply pressure. If the blood spurts, it is from an artery, and pressure with gauze should be applied from above the wound for at least 5 to 10 minutes. If the blood flows, it is from a vein, and pressure should be applied from below for at least 2 minutes. Do not check to see if bleeding has stopped until time has elapsed. Repeat if necessary. Do not dab, or you will disturb the clot.

A wound must be cleaned carefully with warm water. Wet a soft cloth or gauze pad and clean the wound gently from the center of the wound out to the edges. The animal won't like this, but it is an important part of the treatment. Take your time. To be sure any fur, dirt, and feathers stay out of the wound, smear petroleum jelly around, not in, the wound area. The fur or feathers will stick together instead of falling into the wound.

Check carefully for signs of maggots and maggot eggs. Check for overlooked particles and use tweezers or gauze to remove gently.

Once the wound is absolutely clean, dry gently and apply antibiotic cream (or rinse, if the wound is deeper, with Betadine or other antiseptic or antibiotic solution). Hydrogen peroxide is not desirable because of the foaming action. Cover with a clean bandage or a clean, nonstick gauze pad, wrapping this with vet wrap to secure the pad. You may have to secure with tape, but use as little as possible. Do not wrap too tightly or you will constrict breathing or blood supply, particularly with birds.

Once a day, more often if needed, remove the dressing, re-clean the wound, and reapply a fresh dressing.

5.   Infected Wounds and Abscesses

Symptoms and Causes: An existing wound may be contaminated, and become swollen and red. There will be white, yellow, or green pus and fluids in the wound. An abscess is a wound that has closed superficially, lacks air enough to heal, and contains the pus and fluids below the surface. The skin may be swollen and red, will usually feel warm to the touch. An infected wound may smell bad. It may contain maggots.

Treatment: Clean out any maggots or debris. A maggot is the larva of an insect such as a fly. The fly is attracted to an open wound and lays its eggs; within hours, the eggs have hatched to tiny maggots. They do serve a useful purpose by keeping the wound clean and free of infection when they eat dead flesh. They multiply rapidly though, and will eventually penetrate to a vital organ and kill the animal.

To remove maggots from eyes, use sterilized water such as contact lens saline solution. Use an eyedropper to drop the water into the eye, and then suck it back up again. Large maggots will be stuck to the end of the dropper, small ones will be sucked in. Dispose of them and repeat the process.

For maggots on body wounds, flush with saline solution repeatedly. Sometimes a heavy coat of cornstarch will work for a superficial wound. The maggots need a wet area to move freely. When the cornstarch dries, they'll drop off. Then wash off the rest of the cornstarch and treat the wound.

Maggot eggs are yellow, look somewhat like flakes of corn meal, and appear in groups or clumps which are sometimes very large. If the maggot eggs haven't hatched yet, tissue or gauze with petroleum jelly, mineral oil, or olive oil on it will help to remove them. A flea comb will help to get them out of fur. Wash the area well before continuing to treat the wound. Examine the animal several times a day until you are sure all of the maggots are gone. When the wound is free of maggots and debris, coat the fur or feathers around the wound with petroleum jelly, and then clip. This will help to keep the wound clean. Apply hot packs soaked in a solution of 1 pint of hot water with two teaspoons of salt. Keep the pack on the wound 10 minutes at a time and repeat every 2 hours. In the case of an abscess, continue until the abscess opens and drains.

An antibiotic cream can be found in the drug or grocery store (any generic triple antibiotic cream will serve the purpose), and should be applied to the wound. Oral antibiotics such as Amoxicillin, Baytril, or Clavamox should be prescribed by a veterinarian according to the type and weight of the animal.

6. Fractures

Symptoms: There may be obvious deformity or swelling, an inability to use the affected part. Fractures or broken bones require emergency veterinary care. The animal may also be in shock, and may be bleeding. *Do not try to fix without a veterinarian.*

Causes: Car hits, falls, traps, twisting or slipping, gunshots, impact with windows, wires, cruelty.

Treatment: All breaks and fractures should be treated by a veterinarian quickly, but you should stabilize the animal by treating for shock.

A simple fracture has no bone ends protruding. A compound fracture has bone ends protruding through the skin.

Do not try to set or splint a fracture yourself. You will cause more pain than relief and will probably make the fracture worse. If the fracture is compound, control any bleeding. Try not to let anything touch the bone to protect against infection. If possible (the animal may fight you) apply a sterile bandage or gauze pad and wrap lightly where the bones are protruding. Put the animal in a small box so that there is not much room for it to move around. A strong cardboard box or plastic storage bin with holes in the lid for air is a safe container to use. Wire cages or dog carriers may cause further damage to the broken limb. Transport the animal in this container to a veterinarian or rehabilitator.

7. **Poisoning**

Symptoms, Causes, and Treatments: There are many different ways that a mammal or bird can be poisoned. The symptoms may include paralysis, convulsions, excessive salivation, internal bleeding, and hypersensitivity. Treatment differs for different poisons in wildlife just as it does for humans.

It is important that the poison be identified accurately. Animals can be poisoned by pesticides, gases, bee stings, rat poisons, toxic plants, snail or slug bait, lead in paint, antifreeze, household and gardening chemicals, petroleum. Call the animal poison control center at 1-800-548-2423. The idea is to reduce the poison's absorption into the body tissues. A veterinarian may pump the stomach, inject antidotes, or use fluid therapy.

Lead poisoning, for example, is seen in wildlife that swallow lead weights or shotgun pellets along with food. One symptom can be paralysis. Treatment for birds must be professional. Treatment for mammals might be large doses of milk, Epsom salts, or strong tea (call your local wildlife rehabilitator), and transport to a veterinarian.

Pesticides or herbicides used to kill insects or weeds can be ingested. Give a mammal as much milk or water as it will take.

8. Malnutrition and Starvation

Symptoms: In a bird, the breastbone or keel will be sharp to the touch. The breast muscle will be shrunken. In mammals, the body weight will be down, the fur dull and perhaps sparse, the eyes dull, the animal will be weak, listless, puny.

Causes: No food available. Or the animal is too young or too weak to get food for itself.

Treatment: Give the animal rehydration fluid using the methods described under the Dehydration section. If you must keep the animal overnight before getting it to a rehabilitator, feed it small amounts of easily digestible foods such as commercial human liquid diet or prescription dog or cat canned food products for convalescing cats and dogs, which can be gotten from your veterinarian. For birds, you will need to consult a rehabilitator for the proper species-specific diet. You can always begin with bits of peeled grape, watermelon, moistened kibble, moist canned dog or cat food, finger-feeding if necessary.

Proper finger-feeding technique

NOTE: Sometimes starvation is caused by digestive development problems, disease, parasites, or a mechanical cause such a something caught in the throat or a poison. Get advice and help.

9. **External and Internal Parasites**

    Symptoms and Treatment of External Parasites: These can be seen in the fur or feathers of the animal. Feather mites are often difficult to spot on a bird, but if you hold the bird, the warmth of your skin will cause them to travel to your hand where they can be seen and felt.

    External parasites can weaken a compromised animal. Dampen a cloth or paper towel with liquid insecticide such as ParaMist. Pat this over the animal, being careful of the eyes. Start at the neck so that the parasites don't travel to the head. Pull out ticks with tweezers.

    Symptoms and Treatment of Internal Parasites: A great number of animals are carrying internal parasites. They may not be the main problem of the bird or mammal that are dealing with but may make recovery slower. A fecal sample may be examined at a veterinary office, and indicate the presence of parasites or bacteria that can be treated with prescription medicines. Your veterinarian will help you with the type of medications and dosages if you are a licensed wildlife rehabilitator.

10. **Diseases**

Symptoms: Some of these include: apathy, lack of appetite, seizures, paralysis, circling motions, screeching, lack of coordination, runny eyes and nose, diarrhea, and feathers or fur in poor shape. Fever, and a sickly odor, may also indicate a disease.

Treatment: Disease requires a veterinarian. Bring stool samples and all of the information that you have collected about the animal.

Zoonoses: These are diseases wildlife transmits to humans. Rabies, tetanus, psittacosis (from pigeons), and salmonellosis are among them. Baylisascaris procynosis is a roundworm problem found in raccoon feces that can cause severe central nervous system trouble.

If you suspect an animal is diseased, protect yourself and all other animals. Isolate the sick animal and get it promptly to a vet. Wear gloves, wash hands with antibacterial disinfectant soap, and use a disinfectant to wash anything the animal had contact with, especially surfaces contaminated with feces, urine, saliva.

11. **Fever**
Fever is a symptom of disease, parasites, infections, and other problems. Although the fever itself can be treated, the cause of the fever must be found and treated.

12.   Burns and Scalds

Symptoms: Singed feathers or fur, reddening of skin, tissue damage.

Causes: Burns and scalds are caused by direct contact with flames or a hot surface, flying cinders, steam, sparks, hot fluids, cooking oil, hot tar, and caustic chemicals, lightning, live electrical wires.

Treatment: Clean the area with a sterile salt solution or contact lens solution. Apply ice packs or immerse the area in cold water to cool the flesh and help relieve the pain. Put petroleum jelly around the burn and clip the fur or feathers in the area. The jelly will keep fur or feathers from falling onto the injured area. Never use butter, oil, or oil-based ointment on the burn. Apply a cream antibiotic on the site and cover with a nonstick bandage.

13.   Hyperthermia or Heatstroke

Symptoms: Obvious distress, panting, lethargy; animal may have trouble walking, and may stagger and fall if it tries to move. The body temperature will be very high, and there may be convulsions or loss of consciousness.

Causes: Hot environment.

Treatment: Get animal to a cool place, and reduce its body heat. Use cold water, gently poured over the animal, cool cloths or ice packs, get paws or feet into cool water. Keep this up until the animal comes around.

14. Hypothermia or Extreme Cooling of Body Temperature

Symptoms: The body temperature will be very low, the pulse will be weak, and slow. Breathing will be slow and shallow. Skin may feel cool to the touch.

Causes: Cold weather, cold environment.

Treatment: Get animal to a warm place, and begin to warm gradually. Cover with blankets (if small, cup in hands, warm against body). Then place in container or cage. Provide a heat source, such as a heating pad set to low put under 1/3 of the cage or container the animal rests in. A 60 watt light bulb 12" to 18" over a container can provide a steady heat. If frostbite is involved, extremities will become numb. The affected areas may become pale and then turn red and scaly. A bird's feet will be red and swollen. Don't plunge the areas into hot water or rub them. Warm gradually.

15. Diarrhea

Symptoms: Loose or watery stool, sometimes with blood or mucus.

Causes: A bacterial infection, internal parasites, viral infections, overeating or changes in the diet (expect some at first because we will not be able to reproduce natural diet), nervousness or stress, reactions to poisons or heavy metal ingestion, allergy to food or drugs.

Treatment: Pepto Bismol or Kaopectate, doses adjusted to weight of animal. If the diarrhea continues, or has blood in it, check with a vet. You will need a fecal sample done to check for internal parasites, or the vet may recommend an antibacterial, antifungal, or a worming medication.

16. **Bloat (or Constipation)**

Symptoms: Mammal's belly is tight with skin stretched almost to transparency. After feeding, the belly should feel like a marshmallow, not a hard rubber ball.

Causes: Internal parasites, a change in diet, improper diet, overfeeding, or constipation. Also there may be an internal malfunction, as in runtiness (see p. 37).

Treatment: Gas or fecal matter causing the bloat must be expelled. Lay the mammal belly down on a heating pad on low setting or hold a small creature in your hand under warm running water or in a cup bath. Gently but firmly massage from rib cage toward tail. Powdered activated charcoal or powdered calcium carbonate dissolved in water, or small amount of antigas medication such as simethicone may help. Infant gas relief drops are appropriate.

17. **Eyes, Ears, and Noses**

Foreign bodies in eyes may sometimes be removed with a saline wash. If you have no commercial saline solution for eyes, make your own by completely dissolving a teaspoon of salt in a pint of warm water. Saline can also be used to unstick eyelids that have become stuck together. A warm, wet cloth held gently to the eye will also help.

If an animal rubs or shakes its head, or holds its head tilted to one side, paws or scratches the ear, there may be a foreign object in the ear, or there may be earmites present. If the ear seems dirty, clean some of the dirt out and place it on a damp paper towel. If the towel turns red, there are mites present.

There may be dirt in the mouth and nose of an orphaned baby who has been on the ground. Be sure to clean this out before trying to rehydrate or feed.

18.   Runtiness

Symptoms: Low body weight, slow behavioral and physical development, lack of muscle mass, possible sickly and pale appearance—or there may be what seems normal development that suddenly slows or stops. There may be regression.

There are two types of runtiness. In Type 1, the animal shows a behavioral and physical development about one to three weeks behind the normal stages for its age group but is otherwise healthy. These babies are sometimes referred to as late bloomers. In Type 2, the animals will never develop properly. There are abnormalities in the blood, respiratory, and digestive systems based on permanently underdeveloped systems. These babies exhibit loose stools, intestinal gas (bloat), fluid build-up in the abdomen, irregular heart rates, and are pale, sickly, and inactive. Fur is dull, smell is not normal, eyes may not be alert. Long past schedule, these babies continue to urinate on each other, foul the nest and themselves. Weight and development remain retarded. These babies seldom live long; death may be sudden.

Causes: Immature mother, lack of maternal nutrition, unknown causes.

Treatment: Add Nutrical to diet, warmth, watchfulness.

OTHER EMERGENCIES

19. Cat-Caught Animal

Symptoms: Tears in the flesh, punctures (not always visible), crushing injuries in small birds and mammals. Often the victim will appear fine, but don't be fooled. Cat saliva received through an open wound or puncture has potent bacteria that can kill a small creature in 72 hours.

Treatment: Treat for shock. Once the animal is calm, clean the visible wounds and double check carefully to make sure you have found all injuries. Apply topical antibiotics. A veterinarian should administer internal antibiotics as soon as possible and oral antibiotics to continue the treatment for three to five days. Rabbits and deer react badly to oral antibiotics and will need them administered by injection.

20. Air Bubbles

Symptoms: An air bubble may appear under the skin of injured birds. Don't mistake a full crop (on the side of the neck) in some birds for an air bubble. There will be no food visible through the skin of an air bubble.

Causes: An injury will sometimes result in an air leak under the skin.

Treatment: It may deflate on its own. If it does not, and if it is causing pressure or getting in the way of normal movement, have a veterinarian puncture it with a sterile needle, express the air out, and seal the hole with an antibiotic ointment. It may recur within an hour or so, and the procedure must be repeated.

21. Oiled Birds

Symptoms: Oil can be seen on feathers, waterproofing and insulating properties will be gone, bird may be chilled, unable to fly. Waterbirds will not be able to remain afloat.

Causes: Oil spills from shore or tankers on the water.

Treatment: Keep the bird warm through the treatment. Wash out the eyes, mouth, and nostrils. Use Dawn dishwashing liquid in a 5% Dawn to 95% warm water solution. Gently pour the solution over the feathers while stroking in the direction of growth. Do not scrub. Rinse with lots of warm water. Be careful of the eye area. Keep rinsing until water rolls off of the bird in droplets.

Mallard Juvenile

Get the bird to a wildlife rehabilitator. Getting an oiled bird ready for release is complicated and may take weeks of specialized care.

ABUSE AND CRUELTY

Sadly, ours is a species that uses other species for sport and for transferring our own rage. Rehabilitators and veterinarians often receive wildlife that has been stoned, shot at, run over for fun by motorboats, pickup trucks, cars. Animals that are beaten, starved, and generally maltreated must receive care as well as those shot at, downed, but not killed. Please be aware. Please rescue.

5

HANDLING AND RELEASE

Whether the only problem your animal has is being an orphan, or you are temporarily feeding and housing a wounded baby or adult, you will need to know something about diet, housing, and general handling and release techniques.

INITIAL ORPHAN CARE

If the only problem is that this is an orphan baby, otherwise healthy, then put it in a container and keep it warm.

Most babies cannot regulate their own temperatures and need help from a heating pad on low under 1/3 of the container (not inside the container, and only under part of the container so the baby can crawl away from the heat if it wants to). A 60 watt light bulb may be used 12" to 18" above half of the box. Whatever source you use, be sure to check the temperature often. A thermometer is a wise investment.

Mammals

A mammal baby will need to be fed a formula as close as possible to its mother's milk. The size of the infant will determine what kind of feeding instrument to use. You may choose an eyedropper, syringe, kitten-sized feeder bottle, or a regular baby bottle. The baby's first meals will be Pedialyte or other rehydrating fluid. Assume that if it is away from

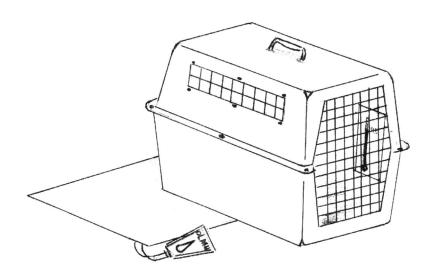

First home for baby mammals

Duckling under teddy and light in brooder.

mom, it is dehydrated. The fluid is also a good transition medium from what the baby has been fed by its mother and the formula it will be given.

Use fluids several times the first hour, then begin to space feedings according to the size of the infant. A tiny baby will usually need to be fed every two hours, a larger baby every four hours. A rehabilitator will begin to introduce formula into the fluids, starting with a 1 part to 4 part mix for a few feedings, then 1 to 3, 1 to 2, and then finally all formula. If at any time there is diarrhea, it is necessary to go back to the previous mix and progress more slowly. Always feed baby mammals on their stomachs, never on their backs to prevent choking and aspiration (inhaling liquid into lungs produces a pneumonia-like condition).

You can get puppy milk replacer or kitten milk replacer from your veterinarian, pet store, or feed and grainstore where animal supplies are sold. As a general rule, squirrels, rabbits, opossum, and woodchuck babies need puppy milk replacer, raccoons need kitten milk replacer.

Baby mammals with their eyes closed need to be stimulated to go to the bathroom after each meal (their mothers lick them in the wild to stimulate and clean). You can do this by gently rubbing the anal/genital area with a soft tissue or a piece of cotton moistened with warm water. Moving about on their blankets will sometimes stimulate the baby enough to release a little urine or stool, but not enough. Once the eyes are opened, this process can be eliminated.

Birds

Baby birds need a nest of some kind to support them. A berry box with scrunched tissues works well, or a ring of twisted paper towels the right size for your birds, with layers of tissues over it. The tissues right under the bird's feet should be scrunched, not smooth, so that the baby does not slip and sprawl. The tissues must be changed often to keep the nest clean.

AGES AND STAGES

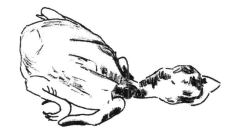

HATCHLING: eyes closed, no feathers: week one

NESTLING: eyes open, hopping, beginning feathers: week 2-3

FLEDGLING: feathered and flying but not self feeding: 25-28 days

Both nestlings and fledglings need to be fed a formula that provides the same food values that its parents provided. A temporary formula can be made from dry cat food or puppy chow soaked in warm water and cut into tiny bits. Baby birds need to be fed about every twenty to thirty minutes, with the time between feedings increasing as the birds gets older. Some birds will gape, some birds need help (gently!) in opening their beaks. You may use tip of finger for larger birds to insert food. For tiny birds, use a swab stick without the cotton. By the time the bird is trying to fly, the feedings will be two hours apart. Please read about the kinds of diet your bird requires in the wild, as the wrong nutrition (feeding grain to an insect-eating or worm-eating bird, for instance) will actually starve it. **Do not feed bread and water. Even in the wild, bread is false calories that make the bird feel full without any nutritional value.** (If you are prone to feed birds as you walk, carry cracked corn in your pocket.)

Get Help

As you can tell, caring for wild young requires training and information. You should get the babies to a trained and licensed rehabilitator who will know the details of this baby's care. If this is not immediately possible, you can find details to help you care for them temporarily in the books from the 7-volume "I Found a Baby" BASIC MANUAL WILDLIFE REHABILITATION SERIES by Dale Carlson, Bick Publishing House. (See order forms in the back of this book.)

Housing

When deciding on housing, choose a cage or container that will make your job of caring for the animal easy. An animal with a wound that needs to be tended to often should be in a cage that allows you to reach the animal without having to chase it each time. An animal with injured legs or wings should be in a small cage or container so that movement is restricted, and the injured part allowed to heal. Make sure that there is nothing in the cage that the animal can hurt itself on. Wire cages are hard on a bird's feathers, especially if the bird is nervous and flutters around each time you approach. **Do not underestimate the ability of wild creatures to escape.**

Wire cages such as a dog cage wrapped in hardware cloth are excellent but cover the wire bottom to protect feet and claws. Newspaper is cheap and absorbent (never use the color parts) and paper toweling can be used to keep the ink from touching the animal. Pine chips, hay, natural materials like soil and leaves are good if there are no open wounds. Pet carriers, plastic boxes with ventilation holes, cardboard boxes, plastic baskets, all these will do.

Wild mammal babies will be comforted by soft cloths to snuggle in and hide under.

Nest boxes are important. They provide comfort, security, and a needed place to hide. A smaller cardboard or wooden box, basket, plastic box will do.

If your animal is older and closer to being ready to be released, the cage should more closely resemble the natural habitat, with branches, leaves, logs, and rocks.

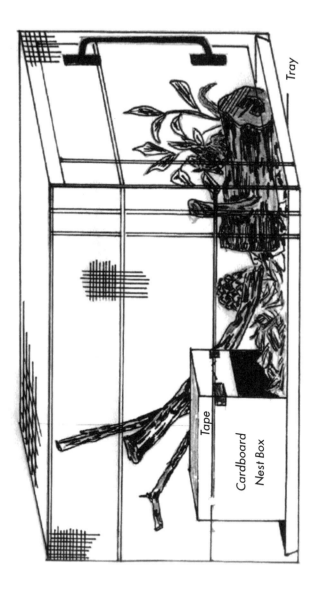

Tray

Tape

Cardboard
Nest Box

Dog crate covered with hardware cloth

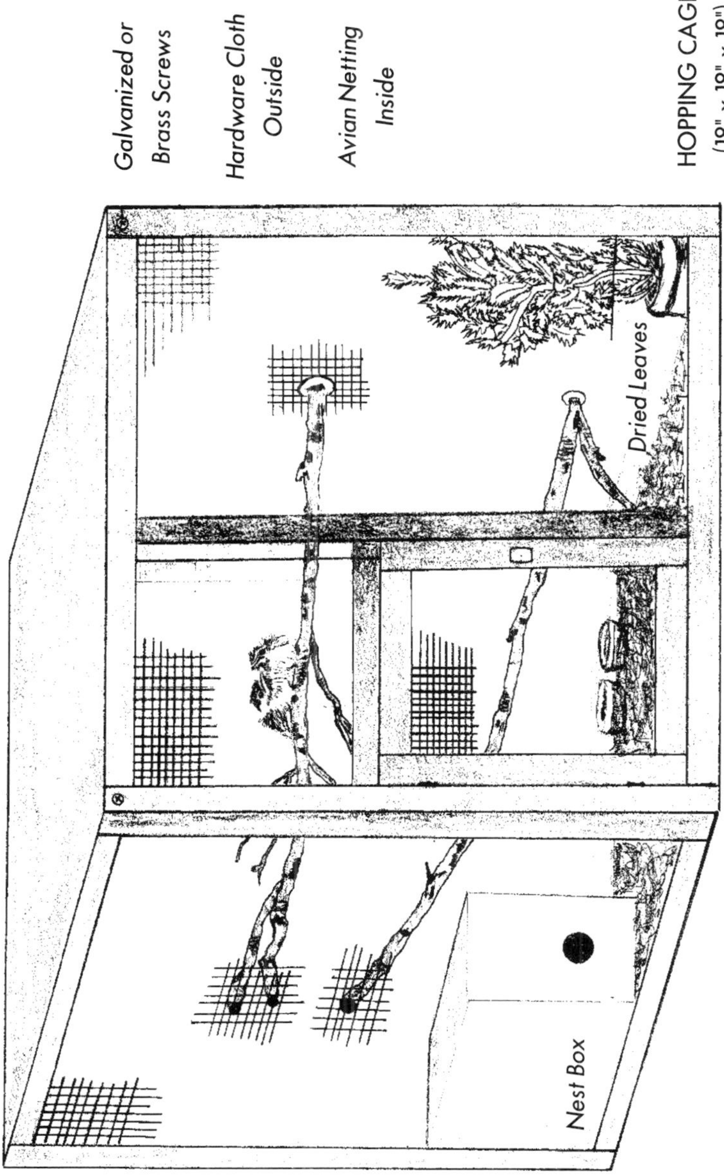

Galvanized or
Brass Screws

Hardware Cloth
Outside

Avian Netting
Inside

HOPPING CAGE
(18" x 18" x 18")

Dried Leaves

Nest Box

OWL CAGE
20' x 10' x 15'

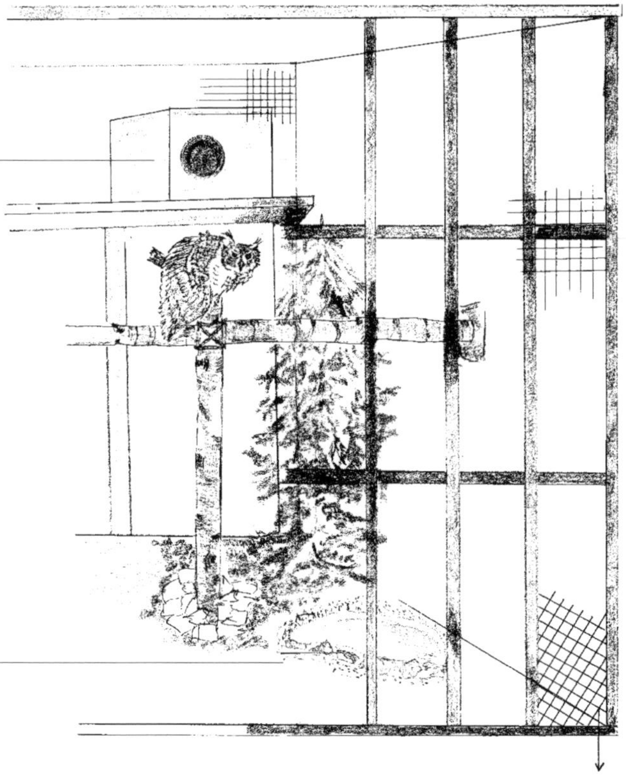

Avian Netting
Inside

Chain Link
Outside

Wire
Underground
18"

Nest Box

Water

Habitat for squirrel, raccoon, or other small mammal.

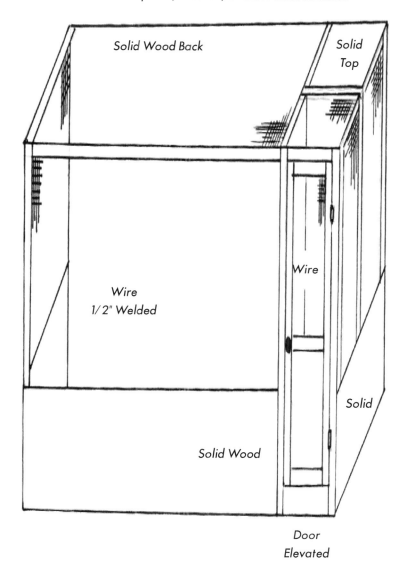

Solid Wood Back

Solid Top

Wire

Wire
1/2" Welded

Solid

Solid Wood

Door
Elevated

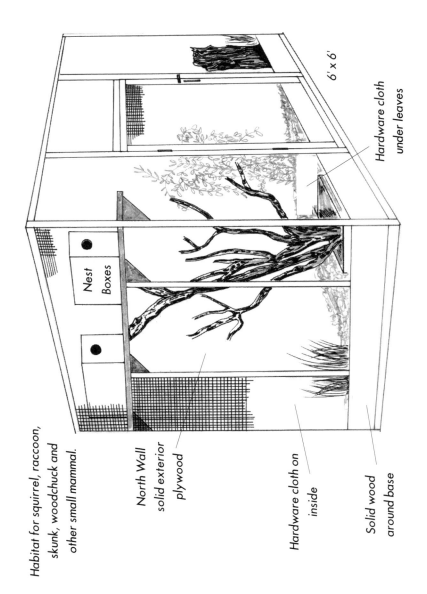

Habitat for squirrel, raccoon, skunk, woodchuck and other small mammal.

North Wall solid exterior plywood

Hardware cloth on inside

Solid wood around base

Nest Boxes

6' x 6'

Hardware cloth under leaves

JUVENILE AND ADULT DIET

Read to find out the natural diet of the adult in the wild and provide an appropriate substitute diet. Poor nutrition will delay healing. Size and shape of the feeding dishes must conform to the needs of the animals. Dog and cat food can always be used as a staple.

Fresh water must be available at all times. Make sure that the water container is the right size and shape for the animal. A tiny bird will have trouble drinking from a large bowl of water. Water bottles fixed to the sides of cages for mammals need to be at the correct height for the mammal to drink comfortably.

RELEASE

Often your emergency first aid will be sufficient to make the animal ready for release. It must be healthy and able to care for itself in the wild. If it is possible and safe, the release site will be the place where you rescued it. The animal is familiar with the place and knows where to find food and water, even its parents or children.

Often the rescue site will not be a safe place and to release the animal there would put it back into a dangerous situation. In that case, choose a new site that has a food supply, water source, and the same species. This will ensure appropriate habitat. Make certain the new site is not too near human habitats, roads, and hunting sites, and is not already too crowded with wildlife. Never release an animal into a tree or hole in the ground. It may be home to a wild critter already.

Make certain of a three-day good weather forecast. Leave a supply of food for at least the first feeding.

6
EUTHANASIA: KINDNESS

Sometimes an animal is so seriously ill or injured that rehabilitation is impossible. Sometimes we are able to save an animal's life but the quality of that life is too sad, painful, unacceptable.

The decision to euthanize an animal ought to be made as objectively as possible. This is easy to do when the illnesses or injuries are devastating. When there is no hope for recovery, the choice is clear. When there is doubt, the decision can be very difficult. Each case will be unique. How to make the decision will be based on an estimation of all the elements of the animal's current health and future prognosis. It will be based on the animal's pain, its ability to survive in its now limited condition, its personal courage, your personal empathy, whether you can do a soft release and keep watch over it, whether it must be released back into the wild on its own. The decision must also be based on your time and workload, the quality of life for the animal, the long-term prognosis, the presence of disease dangerous to its own or other species, including humans, and again, its own level of pain.

It is best not to make the decision alone. Consult with others who are involved with animals, wildlife rehabilitators, your veterinarian. Be part of a group or a network; be affiliated with a rehabilitation center.

Take your time with this decision. Euthanasia cannot be reversed.

Animals that could not survive in the wild without pain and difficulty should be set free with the kindness of euthanasia.

Here are some typical situations where there is no hope for a good life for the animal.

- an animal that cannot feed or care for itself, or is so weak as to be easy prey for predators

- a mammal that has lost two or more legs

- any animal with a break in the spinal cord

- an animal with no bottom jaw

- an animal paralyzed with no sign of improvement after a week of treatment

- any animal suspected of a disease contagious to humans, like leptospirosis and rabies

The goal of euthanasia is to provide a good death, and to end the animal's suffering in the quickest and kindest way possible. **This means to render the animal unconscious before death occurs.**

There are both mechanical and chemical ways to euthanize that are acceptable.

MECHANICAL WAYS

- Gunshot. This requires training to be done so that people and other animals are not endangered and the animal does not suffer. The shot must be directly into the animal's brain.

- Suffocation causes terror, misery, and pain for the animal and is **not** acceptable.

CHEMICAL MEANS: INJECTIONS

Almost always in all states, only veterinarians or licensed personnel are allowed to inject. But injections with any of several death-causing agents are the most kind, efficient, effective method of euthanasia.

Phenobarbital or a mixture of barbiturates and cardiac toxins can be administered. But remember: These and all human medicines require a license to acquire or administer, and must be administered by a veterinarian.

The animal remains are not fit as food when these agents are used and cannot go back into the food chain.

CHEMICAL MEANS: INHALANTS

- Ether. This is effective but explosive. It is obtainable in the form of automobile starter fluid. Rehabilitators who use this put themselves at risk of setting themselves on fire, causing explosions, or endangering their own respiratory states by inhaling some of the fumes. There is also some suffering on the part of the animal.

- CO (carbon monoxide). This is not recommended. It is usually administered via car exhaust, but the animal suffers from the gas by-products, the heat and irritants, before death.

- CO_2 (carbon dioxide). This is the best of the inhalants. It meets the standards for painless death because it renders the animal unconscious rapidly, before respiratory arrest occurs. The American Veterinary Medical Association says this occurs within 6 minutes.

A carbon dioxide chamber does not require extensive training to use properly. A tank of compressed carbon dioxide is connected to the appropriate size container with proper hardware fittings, and the animal placed gently within. CO_2 is very minimally hazardous to us, it is not flammable or explosive, and does not contaminate the animal who can then be buried shallowly and be returned to the food chain.

If this is the method of choice—and you acquire your license as a wildlife rehabilitator—you can contact the International Wildlife Rehabilitation Association, a veterinarian, or a rehabilitator or center for instructions on how to construct a chamber.

Larger Animals

To deal with larger animals, you may ask your local conservation officer to come and kill the animal by shooting it. You may also be able to take the larger animal to the local animal control facility and ask the animal control officer to euthanize it. Check first on the kindness of procedures before you do this.

Now that the choice has been made and carried through in the best way possible, you must begin to deal with your emotions.

Comfort yourself by knowing that you cared enough to help, and that your animal died warm, fed, and safe from fear and predators. James Herriot said on euthanasia in *All Things Wise and Wonderful,* "I hated doing this, painless though it was, but to me there has always been a comfort in the knowledge that the last thing these helpless animals knew was the sound of a friendly voice and the touch of a gentle hand."

7
GRIEF

In the process of caring for wild animals, there are occasions for great happiness, and there are also occasions for sadness and grief.

Grieving is an emotion we experience from a loss. An animal in your care may die and you will feel grief and recognize it as such. Euthanasia, even necessary and done painlessly and efficiently, may cause you to feel grief.

An animal that has done well in your care and has been released may cause you to feel a strong sense of loss. You worry about what will happen to the animal out there without your care. And you miss it.

When you hear of cruelty to animals, and neglect, you feel strong emotions of sadness, anger, and frustration. This is grief. It can combine anger, fear of death, feelings of vulnerability, a sense of loss.

Society does not offer much sympathy to a person grieving about an animal. Your grief is genuine, valid, and painful.

Acknowledge your grief. Talk it over with someone who will understand. Don't let it discourage you, or become self pity or utter tiredness. Accept grief as well as the joy of rescue, and then move on. The wild things need you. They need you to be there ready to help them with the next emergency.

8
MAKE LIFE EASIER FOR WILDLIFE

There are simple things that we humans can do to reduce the casualties, and to make life easier for wildlife.

Plant shrubbery around the edge of your property to give wild animals a place to hide, and to live. These plants could be berry bushes planted just for the wild creatures.

Consider letting part of your yard go wild, leaving logs, brush piles, allowing bramble, vines, undergrowth to flourish as shelter for them.

Put out water for wildlife in all seasons.

If you have free roaming cats, and want to feed birds, make sure that the feeders hang free and are not near bushes where the cats can hide to sneak up on the birds. If you have free roaming cats, seriously consider not feeding birds, or keeping the cats inside. Vets say that people whose cats are outdoors even part of the time spend over twice as much on the care of their cats as people whose cats are indoors. Outdoor cats are victims of car hits, fights with other animals, cuts and scrapes, punctures, poisoning, and parasites. A large percentage of the small birds and mammals brought to rehabilitators are cat caught. Cat saliva has a bacteria in it that is devastating to a small critter and will cause infection and eventually death within 72 hours. Most cats, even those that have spent all of their lives outdoors, can adapt quite well to a life indoors. At the very least, **double-bell** your outdoor cat to give the other critters a chance.

Caps installed on chimneys will keep mammals and birds from nesting in them or coming in out of the cold. Keeping any holes in attics, windows

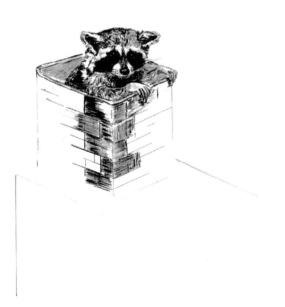

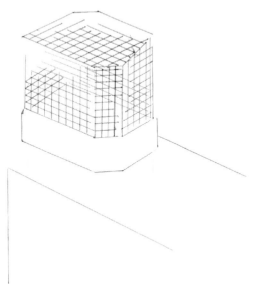

Learn to cap chimneys.

in basements repaired and covered will prevent wildlife from coming in to nest or get warm or find food.

Do not feed your pets outdoors if you don't want to feed wildlife as well. They WILL find the food, they WILL come back for more.

Keep your fences in good repair. Exposed nails, loose wires, and holes in fences are all dangerous to the animals roaming in your area.

Obey road speed limits. Sometimes, go even slower. If there is an area where animals frequently cross, or if the roads are slicker than usual, then reduce your speed even more. Be able to stop or turn to avoid a collision without putting yourself in danger.

When you spot road kill, with your shovel or wearing gloves move it to the side of the road to keep predators from becoming the next victim while feeding.

Secure your trash. Creatures like raccoons are hungry enough and clever enough to eat what they can find.

Be alert for signs of movement on the side of the road when you are driving, and be ready to stop if an animal darts out. At night, watch for pairs of eyes shining with reflected headlights.

Perhaps the most important thing you can do is share with other people your information about animals and animal behavior. Share particularly that animals feel fear and pain, and pleasure and love for their young, just as we do. Advocate for them. The more people understand animals, the more they will show love, respect, and compassion for them.

APPENDIX

REFERENCE BOOKS

Audubon Handbooks, McGraw-Hill Book Company, New York, San Francisco, Singapore, Toronto, et al.

The Merck Veterinary Manual, Merck & Co., Inc., Rahway, New Jersey.

Peterson Field Guide Series, A Field Guide to the Mammals of North America, North of Mexico, A Field Guide to Birds (regional), by Roger Tory Peterson, Houghton, Mifflin Company, Boston.

Stokes Nature Guides, A Guide to Animal Tracking and Behavior, A Guide to Bird Behavior, Volume I, II, III, by Donald Stokes, Little, Brown and Company, Boston.

RECOMMENDED MANUALS

Basic Manual Wildlife Rehabilitation Series (7-VOL), Bick Publishing House, Madison, Connecticut. 203/245-0073.

Basic Wildlife Rehabilitation, IAB, International Wildlife Rehabilitation Council, Suisun, California. 707/864-1761.

Introduction to Wildlife Rehabilitation, National Wildlife Rehabilitators Association, Carpenter Nature Center, Hastings, Minnesota. 612/259-4086.

Wild Animal Care and Rehabilitation, The Kalamazoo Nature Center, Kalamazoo, Michigan. 616/381-2557.

Wildlife Care and Rehabilitation, Brukner Nature Center, Troy, Ohio. 513/698-6493.

Wildlife Rescue, Inc, Austin, Texas. 713/472-WILD.

INDEX

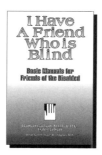

BICK PUBLISHING HOUSE
PRESENTS

7 BASIC MANUALS FOR
WILDLIFE REHABILITATION
by Dale Carlson and Irene Ruth

Step-by-Step Guides • Illustrated • Quick Reference for Wildlife Care
For Parents, Teachers, Librarians who want to
learn and teach basic rehabilitation

*Endorsed by
Veterinarians, Wildlife
Rehabilitation Centers,
and National Wildlife
Magazines*

I Found A Baby Bird, What Do I Do?
ISBN: 1-884158-00-5, $9.25

I Found A Baby Duck, What Do I Do?
ISBN: 1-884158-02-1, $9.25

I Found A Baby Opossum, What Do I Do?
ISBN: 1-884158-06-4, $9.25

I Found A Baby Rabbit, What Do I Do?
ISBN: 1-884158-03-x, $9.25

I Found A Baby Raccoon, What Do I Do?
ISBN: 1-884158-05-6, $9.25

I Found A Baby Squirrel, What Do I Do?
ISBN: 1-884158-01-3, $9.25

First Aid For Wildlife
ISBN: 1-884158-14-5, $9.95

**Wildlife Care For Birds And Mammals
7-Volume Compendium**
ISBN: 1-884158-16-1, $59.70

AVAILABLE AT YOUR LOCAL BOOKSTORE FROM:
**BOOKWORLD, BAKER & TAYLOR BOOK COMPANY,
AND INGRAM BOOK COMPANY**

BICK PUBLISHING HOUSE
307 Neck Road, Madison, CT 06443
203-245-0073

- ❏ I Found A Baby Bird, What Do I Do? $9.25
- ❏ I Found A Baby Duck, What Do I Do? $9.25
- ❏ I Found A Baby Opossum, What Do I Do? $9.25
- ❏ I Found A Baby Rabbit, What Do I Do? $9.25
- ❏ I Found A Baby Raccoon, What Do I Do? $9.25
- ❏ I Found A Baby Squirrel, What Do I Do? $9.25
- ❏ First Aid For Wildlife $9.95
- ❏ Wildlife Care For Birds And Mammals $59.70

Name: _____

Address: _____

Please send check or money order (no cash). Add $3.50 S&H.